GROUND STROKES
IN MATCH PLAY

Here is an instructional tennis book that takes into account all the dynamic, fast-changing elements of the game during match play, when the pressure is really on.

Tennis is a game of quick reflexes, skill, and deception, and Jack Barnaby believes successful contestants constantly modify their play to take advantage of an opponent's weaknesses, the pace of the game, and such factors as wind and court surface. Basics like grips, baseline exchanges, approach and drop shots, and return of service are all covered, and the author's lessons and suggested drills are specifically designed to teach the player how to handle the unexpected while keeping opponents off balance— and winning the match.

Theoretical only where it has to be and illustrated with forty line drawings, this book is a realistic guide that goes beyond technique to the soundest tactics of match play.

GROUND STROKES
IN MATCH PLAY

Techniques, Tempo,
and Winning Tactics

by Jack Barnaby

UNITED STATES TENNIS ASSOCIATION
INSTRUCTIONAL SERIES

Illustrations by George Janes

DOUBLEDAY & COMPANY, INC.
GARDEN CITY, NEW YORK
1978

Library of Congress Cataloging in Publication Data

Barnaby, John M
  Ground strokes in match play.

  (Instructional series)
  1. Tennis. I. Title. II. Series.
GV995.B36   796.34'22
ISBN: 0-385-12705-7
Library of Congress Catalog Card Number 77–16897

Contents

Introduction

The words "ground strokes" as applied to this book, are taken to mean any ball played after it bounces, with the exception of a lob that is bounced and then smashed.

The technique of ground strokes has been explored again and again in tennis literature. What can another book do beyond a rehash with perhaps a few refinements? Strangely, another book can hope to offer a major contribution. Almost all technical tennis writing concentrates on playing the ball out of context, with little or no reference to the place of the stroke within the tactical situation and without regard to that ever-present factor in a match: tempo. These considerations constantly affect technique. The thrust of this book will be to relate technique—even beginner and intermediate —to the ultimate objective: match play at a more advanced level, where the exchanges are faster, styles differ, tempo is seldom absent, deception is important, and one shot often relates so closely to the next that separating them is unrealistic in teaching or learning. This is an approach to ground strokes that has seldom if ever been thoroughly explored, and while in a game as complex as tennis the last word is never spoken, it is hoped to stimulate everyone's thinking with the objective of more realism: Each stroke will be considered as it is used in fast play, in the context of a match.

Perhaps one common example will suffice. Tennis players often assert that tennis is like golf—one is merely playing a different ball with a different stroking instrument. This is very far from the truth. The games are scarcely comparable! There is no tempo at all in golf. The ball sits there, awaiting your pleasure. You have all the time you want for a deliberate careful backswing—as big a one as you may find desirable. In tennis, the ball comes flying at you, often very quickly so your available time is near zero. In golf, you play the ball and stand there, watching its flight or watching it roll toward the cup on the green. In tennis, starting back to position must be instantaneous, literally a part of your stroking technique, or you may not be ready for the next shot. In golf there is no deception. If you make a good shot there is nothing an opponent can do about it. In tennis, a fine lob, an excellent passing shot, a good approach shot, or a good drop shot—all are to little avail if your opponent can read you and get the jump on the ball. Deception—hiding your shot until the instant of actually playing it—is often an essential to success in both offense and defense. All these considerations have quite drastic effects on technique: how you play the ball. The open stance is invalid in golf, but perfectly valid in tennis since it aids markedly in recovery of position. The length of your backswing in tennis must be severely limited if the ball comes fast, as when receiving a hard service. It is not a matter of what you'd like to do, it is a matter of how much you *can* do in the half second or less you have before the hard service is past you. You may prefer to take your time, let the ball pass the top of its bounce, and play it on the way down (very advisable for beginners). But in advanced play if a server is following to net, tactics dictate that you must not let him get way in. You *must* take the ball early. This changes the time available, the length of your swing, and the aspect (slant) of the racket face. Your entire stroking technique is at once altered by a compelling tactical consideration.

This then is the purpose of this book: to relate technique constantly to actual playing situations and to emphasize how these considerations modify technique, often far more markedly than is generally recognized. All players and teachers are reminded of the old saw, "The proof of the pudding is in the eating." Often a conception of a stroke—with an elliptical backswing, careful step-into-it footwork, good weight transfer, perfect contact point, and full follow-through—will read beautifully. But, what happens in a match when the tempo is high? Let's look at it realistically, not theoretically.

GROUND STROKES
IN MATCH PLAY

I

Ground Strokes for Beginners

Grips should relate to the structure of the human body and its appendages; namely, arms and legs. Our considerations should be anatomical rather than imitative of a current winner. How are we best designed to function?

A forehand is an action executed by the fore of the hand; that is, the palm. The most natural way to do this is with the flat of the palm. If the racket is held so that the face of the racket is in the same plane as the palm, we get an eastern grip (Figure 1). We get a western grip (Figure 2) when the racket is turned over (face down) compared to the palm. We get a continental grip (Figure 3) when the racket is opened (face up) compared to the palm. Obviously, the racket can be held slightly or decisively turned over or opened, so we refer to such grips as "a slight continental" or "an extreme western" or "a full continental." Basically, if the racket is over, a little or a lot, when the palm is perpen-

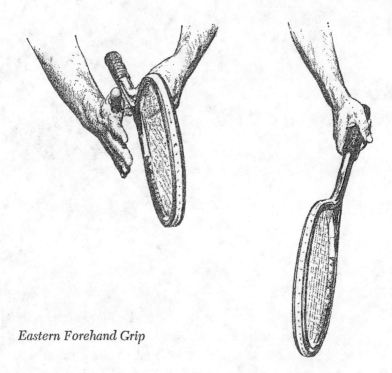

Eastern Forehand Grip

Note that the palm of the hand and the face of the racket are in the same plane.

dicular, we have some kind of a western grip. When the racket is open, a little or a lot, when the palm is perpendicular, we have some kind of a continental. When both are perpendicular—in the same plane—we have a true eastern in which the racket face is actually a continuation of the palm.

The average ground stroke is played with the face of the racket nearly perpendicular to the ground. With an eastern grip the racket is slanted correctly without any distortion of what we can call "the most natural swing." By contrast, a western grip requires us to open the palm to get a perpendicular racket face, and the continental grip requires us to close the palm in order to get a perpendicular racket face. Thus, these grips force us to depart from the easiest most natural swing. This can be done, and is done, by many players. But it is more difficult, takes longer to learn, and is therefore not advisable for beginners.

2A

2B

Western Forehand Grip

The hand is open (slightly palm up) compared to the perpendicular racket face.

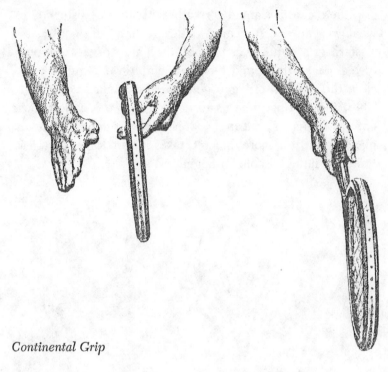

Continental Grip

The hand is closed (slightly palm down) compared to the perpendicular racket face.

There is another consideration that is important. For a high ball we may wish to close the racket face somewhat. This is very difficult to do with a continental grip, since now the distortion from the natural swing becomes almost intolerable—that is, very uncomfortable. It is, therefore, no wonder that people with continental forehands are notoriously mediocre in their ability to drive a high-bounding ball. In the same way, the western grip makes it very difficult to

open the racket face to play a low ball. The eastern grip
allows one to play high, low, or average balls, all with ease—
i.e., with minimum distortion of our swing.

There is yet one more factor that drastically enforces the
statement that the eastern forehand grip is best. We all wish
to get our weight into the shot, both for pace and a feeling
of security in having the shot thus backed up by our heft.
With an eastern grip the ball can be taken off the front foot
and the weight can come in behind it. Also, the rod of our
arm is braced right into the back of the racket, totally rein-
forcing the pressure we are applying to the ball. By contrast,
a player with a continental grip *must* take the ball later—
more by the belt buckle—or the ball will go too high. Try it.
It is very uncomfortable to take a ball early with a continental grip without having the face of the racket too open.
In sum, we can't do it, so we take the ball later for comfort.
The result is that we are pulling the shot rather than pushing it. There is little behind the ball—the rod of the arm hits
the top of the handle rather than the back. Therefore, on
those rare occasions when a person with a continental grip
has a good forehand (Rod Laver, for one), it is because he
has an exceptionally strong and educated wrist. The vast
majority of average players will fail where he succeeded because of these unavoidable facts. (By "average players" is
meant even quite good ones, not just the worst.)

The western grip allows one to take the ball early and
therefore hit very hard. But the racket face is closed, and a
good bit of extra energy must be expended to get the ball up
over the net. Most successful westerns are owned by people of tremendous energy: Little Bill Johnston back in the
early twenties on up to Björn Borg today hit with great
ferocity. If one is that energetic and can train to sustain the
effort through a match, then it can be a lethal way to play

the ball. This, like the great wrist required for the continental forehand, is a special attribute that the general run of players don't possess.

The above reasoning is what is behind the fact that the vast majority of teaching professionals advocate the eastern grip for the forehand ground stroke. The preference is based on sound biomechanics—the way we are built to function most easily and efficiently.

RIGHT AND WRONG

This does not mean that it is wrong to play the ball any other way. It does mean that this is the *easiest* way to do the job; therefore is recommended to all as the best way to start out when taking up the game. It does mean that one can develop a good forehand without putting on one's self the extra demands that go with varying either way from this norm. It does mean that teachers will do well to think twice before espousing any other forehand grip in their instruction of beginners. It does mean that it is no coincidence that the greatest base-line forehands have been easterns, and no coincidence that the Australians, who as a group have favored the continental, are far more famous for their backhands than for their forehands (Rosewall and Sedgman being two great examples).

THE BACKHAND GRIP

Again we have the three categories: eastern, western, and continental. But we do not play a backhand with the back of our hand. We play it with the edge or heel, as in karate.

Therefore, the hand should be on top of the racket, with the thumb half-turned behind the handle.

Try pounding a wall, backhanded, at a height slightly above the knees. The fist will be clenched, the wrist will be comfortably cocked, and the blow will be dealt with the edge of the hand (Figure 4 A). This is the strongest fighting position of the arm and hand in dealing a backhanded blow. For contrast, try hitting the wall with the back of the hand. Watch out: You'll hurt yourself (Figure 4B).

4A   *Dealing a Backhanded Blow*

4B

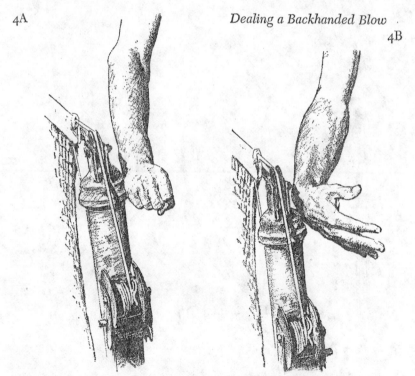

A: Correct: Wrist comfortably cocked, blow dealt with the edge of the hand, as in karate.

B: Incorrect: Blow dealt with back of hand; the weakest way to hit backhanded.

Now, with the hand in this fighting position, put the racket in it with the face just a hair open. You will have an eastern grip. Open the face more, without changing the hand (change the racket), and you will have a continental grip. Again, without changing the hand, close the face a little past the perpendicular: the result is a western grip. Look closely at Figures 5A, 5B, 5C.

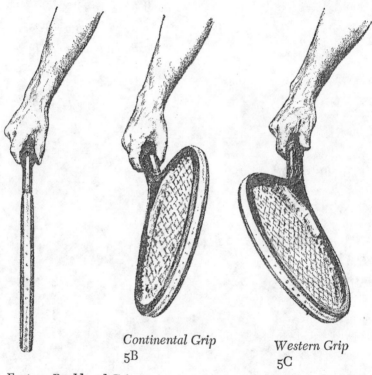

Continental Grip
5B

Western Grip
5C

5A *Eastern Backhand Grip*

Note that exactly as with the forehand grips (with the hand in its natural position) the eastern grip yields a perpendicular racket face; the continental, an open face; the western, a closed face.

Again the eastern grip is the happy mean, the continental tends to be too open, the western too closed. All the reasons for preferring the eastern grip for the forehand are equally valid for the backhand, so there is no need to repeat them, except to point out that the greatest backhand of all time was that of J. Donald Budge, who used (and now teaches) an eastern grip.

VARIETY IN GRIPS

At times during play it is necessary to change the aspect of the racket face to play a certain shot. There are two means of accomplishing this: Change the aspect of the hand or change the grip. Small changes can be affected easily by changing the hand, and no grip change is necessary. But there are occasions when the hand cannot be changed enough: Then the grip must change. Note that word "must"—meaning there is no choice. Typical examples are retrieve and lob situations, when the ball has got a little behind the retriever and is low. On both forehand and back-it is physically impossible to make the shot with standard grips. On the forehand it is necessary to change to an extreme continental that is roughly the same as an eastern backhand. On the backhand it is necessary to use an eastern or slightly western forehand grip. In both cases the change opens the racket face until it is just about horizontal, so the "get" will be, hopefully, a high lob. Note the grip in Figure 6, and if you wish, try this with an ordinary grip. You can't do it. The only way is to make a drastic grip change.

A continental grip tends to open the face, so with a natural swing, the bottom edge of the racket tends to lead as

6　*Forehand Retrieve*

Note the grip, which is changed radically. Why? Because of the need to play with a flat, open, racket face—impossible with any orthodox forehand grip. In the same way, a backhand retrieve requires a drastic change. There are many other instances where a grip change facilitates a special purpose. All good players—including those who assert they never change their grips—use these tricks, consciously or unconsciously.

the racket leaves the ball. The continental is, therefore, very good for slicing. Many players will use two grips on each side—an eastern for a topspin drive; a continental for a sliced shot. This is optional, because one *can* slice with eastern grips. But many players find it easier to make a very slight grip change to facilitate achieving a desired spin. It becomes so habitual that many don't know they do it—but they do. This, of course, is not for beginners, but intermediates and advanced players should be taught to chop and slice, since these are indispensable skills, and if a slight (one-eighth or one-quarter inch?) grip change helps them do it, it should be encouraged, not discouraged.

A very good example is the service. The service is a gigantic chop shot. The continental grip facilitates cutting, so we teach that grip for service, since it is easy to lead with the bottom or right-hand edge of the racket and get a lot of spin. The difficulty of producing the desired spin with an eastern grip verges on the impossible—almost zero good players use the eastern or western grip for service.

The fundamental principle is that the arm wishes to or is built to operate in a certain way. We can't change that much—it's the way the Lord made us. The racket can be held any way we like. It can be changed all we want whenever we want. Many players use a slight continental for a hard service (less spin) and a more full continental for topspin and twist (more spin). While change for the sake of change introduces unnecessary and undesirable complexity, nevertheless it is a great fallacy, and unfortunately a popular one, to assert that there is one right grip and all others should be shunned. If a player can make his service (a forehand shot) with one grip and his forehand drive with another—and thousands do this—doesn't this prove at once that variety is possible, desirable, and can be mastered? If the above is admitted as true, then why can't they use two grips on their backhand? Yet people shrink from the thought as too complicated. Then they will go right ahead and try to use a separate grip at net—one that is different from their drive grips. Thus, they are admitting that variety is necessary and can be achieved. But simultaneously they refuse to consider any variety at the net as too complicated. This kind of thinking keeps contradicting itself. What sense does it make to assert a player can vary his forehand grip for the service but not from topspin to slice drive; he can't vary his backhand grip at the base line but can use a different grip at net; once at the net he can't vary at all, not even between forehand and backhand? It is as though we were metronomes, saying, "I can, I can't" with each swing of the pendulum. These statements have no basis in logic and should be classified as popular myths.

The logical facts would seem to be: We should allow our body to function naturally, and the racket should be accommodated to our physique, not vice versa since that is often awkward, difficult, sometimes even impossible. We should strive for simplicity by limiting these changes to a minimum, but we should admit that tennis is complex enough so that total elimination of changes is impossible. Whenever the body and arm cannot make a change comfortably, the racket should be changed. This applies all over the court—at the base line, the half court, and at net. The fact that play is faster at net makes no difference at all in the facts of our physique. Whether we must learn to execute slowly, with all the time we want (as in service), or quickly (as at net), the limitations of our body and arm and hand are exactly the same. The racket must be adjusted (by a grip change) if the physique cannot comfortably do the job at hand.

FEEL IN THE GRIP

All grips should be diagonal in the hand. The grip covers four or five inches of the handle. The rear part of this should be solidly against the upper palm so the rod of the arm gets a firm connection with the racket. The front part should go diagonally across the palm so it gets onto the fingers, giving a feeling of skill and touch. Figures 7A and 7B show right and wrong. It is important for beginners to learn this distinction, otherwise they may "club" the racket clumsily and progress slowly.

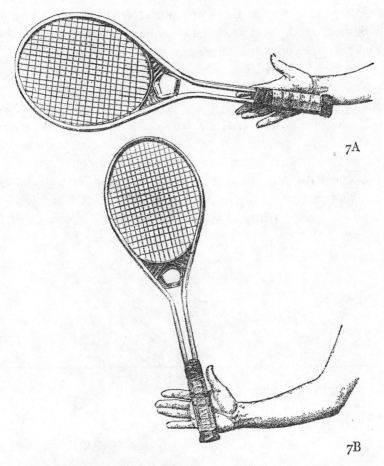

Good Drive Grips Are Diagonal

Note how the racket is scarcely cocked at all: It is almost a direct continuation of the arm. To achieve this effect and "finger feel," the racket must be very diagonal as in 7A. The racket should be cocked sharply, as in 7B, only when we wish to chop the ball (as in service), some volleys, and overhead. The same is true for backhands.

Feel in any grip is there because rapport has been established, via the grip, between the mind and the face of the racket. A player with feel knows—senses—exactly how his racket face is slanted without looking at it. After all, he can't look at it: He must watch the ball. On the forehand he feels the back flatness of the handle. This is in the same plane as the face of the racket. If he feels this, he knows. If he doesn't feel it, the ball may go unexpectedly high or low—he doesn't know. On the backhand the side of the thumb is on the back flatness of the handle, and the second joint of the forefinger is against the front flatness. Both these flatnesses are in the same plane as the strings. Figure 8 shows one

8

Learning to Feel a Backhand

Use just the thumb and fore-finger, feeling the front and back flatnesses of the handle that are in the same plane as the racket face. This is your "rapport" with the strings.

good way to develop this feel—by using only the two fingers.

A beginner would do well to experiment—with a motionless ball—on getting this feel of putting the racket face squarely onto the ball. The wildness of beginners is largely due to lack of feel, since they have no sense of the aspect of the racket face. There is a great and quite understandable eagerness to get right into playing the ball. This should be tempered by a realization that permanently mediocre technique is very often due to starting out, in a hurry, with little or no attention to that most basic of basics—the grip. Its importance cannot possibly be overemphasized, since it is the foundation stone of all future technical skills.

CHANGING GRIPS: USE TWO HANDS

People often have great difficulty with this, particularly at net. There are two reasons for this frustration. They try to do it with one hand, and they change the position of the hand rather than the racket.

To change with one hand is indeed difficult. The grip must be loosened, or how can it change? But this means, when using only one hand, that you practically drop the racket. To avoid this the racket is lifted a bit and quickly grabbed again with the new hold before it has time to fall out of the hand. The result is a quick jiggling effect that is difficult even when you're on the base line and impossible in fast net play. This is why so many people say, "I can't change at net—I don't have time." If they use one hand, they are correct: They definitely don't have time.

If the racket is held at the throat with the left hand, pointed straight out from the stomach, one will naturally have an eastern forehand grip with the right hand. If the left hand pulls the racket head to the left about ninety degrees, so it is parallel to the stomach, and the right hand does *nothing* except stay there loosely allowing the racket handle to alter its position relative to the hand, the butt will swing under the hand toward the little finger and the grip is changed. Study Figures 9–11 closely: The right hand allows

To Change Grips:
Use Two Hands

The right hand relaxes and does nothing, merely allows the left to pull the racket head around about 90 degrees (Figure 10). This swivels the butt under the right hand—the grip is changed (Figure 11). As this is done the racket is simultaneously pulled toward the ball, so zero loss of time occurs. The most difficult part of the skill to acquire is the looseness of the right hand. If the right is tight, how can the left affect a change?

9

the butt to push under, so the right hand turns onto the top of the racket into the strongest backhand position. The left hand does all the work and actually also pulls the racket to the left so that the grip change and the backswing are accomplished in one motion—which is just as quick as using one grip. There is no lost time at all.

10   11

By contrast, if the racket is balanced by the left hand and the right hand is moved over the top of the racket before the backswing is begun, we have two things to accomplish sequentially. When the ball comes fast, this takes too long—particularly at net, but also in receiving hard services.

It seems a bit like the question, "Which came first, the chicken or the egg?" Does it matter whether we change the racket or change the hand? It matters a great deal, because the backswing (preparing the racket to meet the ball whether there is any "swing" or not) must start instantly, not after we do something else such as change the grip or move our feet. Thus, it is crucial to realize that the left hand changes the racket's position in the right hand and moves it to the left, starting the backswing. The right hand does not change its position on the handle and then, later, start the backswing. It seems like a fine point, but at high tempo microseconds make the difference. With beginners it doesn't matter, but they should learn a method of play that will later prove serviceable under stress.

A good way to practice this is to change the racket forehand to backhand to forehand, etc., with a limp right hand on the butt. It will be found the right hand has to help a little by rotating from palm perpendicular (forehand) to palm flat over (backhand), but the rotation of the butt will tend to force this to happen and little initiative is required from the right hand. Drilling on this two-handed switching is very rewarding. If it is done very slowly at first to get it right, it will soon develop into a habitual reflex that is quick as a flash and requires no thought at all. The foundation for excellence at a high level of play has been laid.

The grip-change skill should be practiced without any footwork at first so there is no diversion of concentration.

When it is reasonably mastered (and not before), the footwork can be co-ordinated with it since in the long run everything starts at once.

Why is the racket skill put ahead of footwork? Because in high-tempo play, such as receiving a fast service, one can play the ball without "getting sideways" or "stepping in." But one cannot play without preparing the racket to meet the ball. Watch a fast net exchange in doubles: There is usually no footwork at all, because there isn't time for it. It is all racket work. This is the one indispensable, so put it first all the time so it becomes a habit. Again, a foundation for future excellence has been laid at the beginner level, and a player's possible improvement is limited only by his intrinsic potential, not by his manner of going about it.

TACTICS

A beginner is happy to get the ball into the court. He should concentrate exclusively on not losing the point, never mind winning it. His tactics should be to play quite gently—never hit hard—so the ball will seldom go out. He should play up, aiming four feet or more above the net, so he develops the habit of missing the net rather than frequently hitting it. He should aim at the largest possible target, the middle of the whole court. Thus he gives himself the least risk of hitting too long, too short, too low, or too much to either side. This is percentage play for a beginner. It can be summed up by saying, "Play gently, play up, play cross-court from the sides, play down the center from the center." In a game as tough as tennis, this is a burden enough, and allows the beginner to concentrate on the mechanics that must be mastered before any more ambitious tactics are undertaken.

THE STROKES

There are several problems involved: the grip, racket preparation, balance, timing, and the actual playing of the ball. If a beginner will position himself properly before he tosses the ball and check his grip and racket preparation before he tosses, he has taken care of grip, preparation, and balance, and can put his mind on timing and playing the ball. Note in Figure 12 on page 22 the slight crouch, the pointed left foot, the eastern grip, the slightly open face, the abbreviated backswing, the ball held palm up directly above the point where it will bounce. He should now toss the ball about head high, wait for it to bounce up, and play it just as it starts down.

Why toss it head high? Why not throw it down or drop it? Because we are trying to duplicate the conditions of actual play even while making it easy (note footwork has not even been mentioned beyond stance). In real play an opponent's shot rises up over the net, falls down, bounces up, and starts down again: Then we play it. If the ball is tossed up by the left hand so it goes up, down, up, and starts down before we play it, then we have re-created everything that occurs in a real exchange except the horizontal motion of the ball. We must *wait* before we play—wait for it to go up, stop, and start down. This is timing—withholding the stroke until the proper time. This is an act of selection that is baffling to many beginners. They must learn that they cannot swing any old time, but must wait for the best time; i.e., when the ball is almost motionless, after all the jumpiness of the bounce has been canceled by gravity. A ball that bounces does not merely go up and down. It goes up, *stops,* and goes down. Once it has stopped it is easy to play, hard to miss. While it is jumping up it is easy to miss. Taking the ball on the rise is not for beginners—it is too difficult by far.

The last problem is the shot itself—playing the ball. All the rest is preparatory. The racket, coming from behind and slightly below the ball, should carry the ball forward and up so it will clear the net by a wide margin (four feet?). The motion must be as smooth as possible. A beginner often thinks he has to *hit* the ball. His mental image is one of whacking it hard and suddenly. Of course it flies all over the place. If he can think, "Come to the ball slowly and *press* it," he will eliminate the jittery stroke and cut down the wild speed.

Most importantly, he will learn to aim. To aim means to control, to guide as contrasted with banging the ball and then looking to see where it went. This guiding implies that we stay on the ball for quite a while, carrying it along the path we wish it to take before we let it go off on its own. If the beginner thinks of this, he will soon learn to do it. If he thinks of whacking it he will whack it. This is why we say, "Stay with the ball as long as you can: press out forward and up a little to guide it over the net." This concept of a play that takes time as contrasted with an instantaneous hit is what leads to the more advanced concept of *stroke.* As always, we are building toward the final objective, advanced play, even though nothing has been said about spin, and shouldn't be said at such an early stage.

Beginner Forehand

Details are important. Figure 12: eastern grip, *not* cocked up, comfortable crouch, bent knees, pointed left foot, square stance, slightly open racket face. Get all these right *before* tossing the ball. Figure 13: Toss ball up (do not drop it or throw it down). Toss it at least head high so it will bounce up comfortably high or a bit more. Toss it directly above the proposed point of con-

tact, so its motion is all perpendicular. Figure 14: Contact. Note the ball is taken at the most comfortable height for the player —that is, where the arm hangs naturally. Figure 15: Follow through high to carry ball well above net. A beginner's drive resembles a low lob. Racket face should be perpendicular at top of follow-through.

There are two problems that are the most common with beginners in trying to implement this concept. The hand and arm have three sections and three joints. The upper arm is joined at the shoulder and elbow; the lower arm at the elbow and wrist, the hand at the wrist. This is a rather complicated mechanism. Beginners tend to flap the wrist, or follow through with the lower arm only by bending the elbow. In sum, their swing is unco-ordinated. If a beginner will hold his racket out to the forehand side and experiment, he will soon achieve understanding. Swing and flap the wrist. Swing and bend the elbow excessively. Then swing using only the shoulder joint and see how it all smooths out. The differences and meaning then begin to clear up and progress is spurred.

The second problem concerns the racket. A beginner may prepare very nicely, but as he carries through his racket turns over and he hits the net; or his racket opens and the ball pops up. He must control the slant of the racket face all the way to the end of the follow-through. Otherwise his preparation is undone, and he has spoiled what could have been a nice shot. Stressing the follow-through helps markedly with this problem. Anything that happens in the follow-through begins farther back; that is, while the racket is playing the ball. Therefore, if a beginner will swing forward and up and concentrate on having his racket face perpendicular to the ground when he finishes, such problems will tend to be eliminated. It helps for such a player to swing a few times very slowly, without the ball, prepare his racket properly, and then as he swings to tell himself, "Keep it that way, keep it that way," all the way to the very finish. He should be straightened out, and no longer roll over or slither under.

Nothing has been said about weight transfer. Little or nothing needs to be said. If a beginner tries to stay with the ball and carry it, press it, guide it, he will lean and transfer his weight because he has to. He can't stay on the ball unless he does. So the concept of weight transfer is implicit in the other instructions given and need not be stressed separately, unless a beginner stands perfectly still and doesn't lean at all. Even then, it is often because he is stiff and straight, and if he will crouch (i.e., don't be stiff but bend the knees and waist), he will start to glide his weight with the swing. Many times the tension of trying hard stiffens beginners, so they have this fault. As they get a little better and relax and don't make such an earth-shaking project out of it, they become more fluent and "let it happen," says Tim Gallwey, author of *Inner Tennis*. Their weight begins to transfer as it wanted to all along except that their worried rigidity prevented it.

For many purposes "a picture is worth a thousand words." The reader is directed to Figures 12–15 to fill in wherever the words are inadequate. But a clear concept of what the pictures are showing will enhance their value. The pictures offer a method for every shot: racket ready, wait, play. It could be rephrased to say, "Prepare, time it, play."

The pictures also show two differences on the backhand (Figures 16–19). The racket is held out at the contact point until the ball is tossed, then it is taken back with two hands. This is because it is very awkward to put the racket back with the right arm and cross the left way over to toss the ball out front. The grip, stance, and aspect of the racket are all prepared before the toss. The second difference is the contact point, which is the width of the shoulders farther forward than the forehand. This is merely because

Practice Backhand

Important details: Figure 16: Ball is held palm up (not palm down) above (not below) the racket, directly above spot where it will bounce, so toss and action of ball will be vertical. Figure 17: Ball is tossed head high and racket taken back with two hands (left hand at the throat). Figure 18: Contact. Left hand has helped racket start forward, but does not grip racket: The fingers are open so racket can leave left hand without hindrance. Figure 19: High follow-through for good net clearance.

we are playing the ball with the arm that is hung in front instead of with the back arm, as in the forehand. In each case the ball is played diagonally in front of that shoulder from which the playing arm is hung, so there is basically no difference.

Everything else that has been said about the forehand applies equally to the backhand. This deserves a little stress.

It simplifies technique if we realize that there is literally no difference at all between a forehand and a backhand. After all, what the racket face (the strings) must do to propel a sphere—a ball—through a gas—air—and control its flight is a matter of physics and doesn't change just because you stand on the other side of the ball. If a player were hung by the ankles by a rope attached to the ceiling, the racket face would still have to do the same things to get the same result. The player might have trouble from his bizarre "stance"— weight transfer would be difficult—but he would still be trying to do the same thing, however awkwardly.

The Two-handed Backhand

Figure 20: The most common two-handed grip. Each hand has an eastern forehand grip. Since this is an extremely weak way to use the right hand (see Figure 4B, page 7), it is apparent that most of the strength comes from the left-handed forehand. It really isn't a backhand at all.

20

THE TWO-HANDED BACKHAND

This has come into great vogue in recent years. (Figures 20, 21). Actually there are very few true two-handed backhands. The majority are a left-handed forehand aided a little (very little) by the right hand which stays on the racket with a forehand grip and therefore is of very little help. A real two-handed backhand would be made with the right hand changed to a backhand grip and the left hand with a

Figure 21: In this illustration, the right hand has moved over the top of the racket into a continental grip so it can contribute to the power of the shot. While this would seem to be the most logical way to get the most from two hands, it is seldom seen. Why? Because most uninstructed beginners try to play the backhand with their forehand grip, feel weak, and put their left hand behind the racket to bolster it. There they are with the grip shown in Figure 20, giving them a left-handed eastern forehand.

21

forehand grip, but very few players do this. Most make the shot without changing their right hand at all. It is thus of little use, since nothing but the finger tips are behind the racket. Their stroke is, in fact, a plain eastern forehand played with the left hand.

This approach is very useful to people with weak wrists who cannot get enough strength with their backhand. The reinforcement of the left hand and arm gives them firm security and strength where before they tended to be wobbly and weak, even when they executed rather well. In particular, young girls who cannot do much at all on the backhand side with one hand can make a marked improvement using two, because they suddenly have the needed strength.

The drawbacks are that one's reach and follow-through are restricted (the rear arm won't go as far as the front arm). Players therefore must get closer to the ball to play it, which in itself necessitates faster footwork. The shorter follow-through makes for a very compact swing, with an increased body turn to compensate for less arm motion. But it is apparent that weak-wristed players are better off with the two-handed stroke, and gain far more than they lose by espousing it. For the very top players, both methods seem to be effective since there are great backhands with both techniques.

The important aspect is to realize that the two-handed backhand is essentially a forehand stroke. Therefore, particular attention should be paid to the left hand, its grip, preparing the racket face with the proper slant, and keeping it that way throughout, just as with a one-handed technique. As has been pointed out, the physics involved is unchangeable: A six-handed player from Mars would still have to make the racket execute the same motions.

DIFFERENCES

Surely someone will say, "This fellow's stroke doesn't resemble that fellow's at all—yet they both have good strokes." What varies is, first, personal mannerisms. Alice Marble (one of the all-time great backhands) took her racket back rather low. Chris Evert takes it back above her left shoulder. But she then *drops* it almost to the ground so that she comes to the ball from below, with the racket face perpendicular or a hair open—exactly as Alice Marble did. The two strokes look different, but they are the same. Björn Borg goes through amazing flourishes with his forehand before he gets to the ball—he looks as different as one could imagine—but when he gets there, actually on the ball, his racket face is correct and he doesn't miss very often. Some people use circular swings, some more elliptical, some plain straight back and forth, some bend their arm more than others in preparing or backswinging, but the real core technique (the face of the racket while it is on the ball) cannot vary very much without resulting in inferior stroke production.

Second, on the backhand particularly, some players use topspin and some use slice. Now there is a legitimate difference since the two techniques accomplish two different things. Rosewall uses a rather flat slice and does it very well, so his backhand is good. Don Budge used topspin and had a great backhand. So Rosewall swings straight forward through the ball while Budge followed through high above his head. If one put topspin on the ball with Rosewall's swing, the ball would hit the net. If one sliced with Budge's swing, the ball would probably go over the fence.

There can be slight variations of the same technique. One can use more or less topspin, or more or less slice. This again will make strokes look different. But topspin strokes go from low to high, and cut strokes, from high to low. Personal mannerisms and changes in the degree of spin don't change these fundamentals, which are what really concern us.

PRACTICE: USE A WALL

There is no substitute for constant repetition to create muscle habits. The first objective of any person learning the game should be to find out how to practice by himself. The procedure outlined in the preceding paragraphs (stance, toss, time it, play) is one tried-and-true method. If some kind of a practice wall is available, anyone can develop a degree of competence and the confidence that comes with it without needing a court or a partner. People tend to say, "There is no practice wall available." This is just not true. The side of a garage, the back steps, the wall (inside or out) of a gymnasium, or a purchased rebound net—anything will do. There are even soft balls available that can be hit hard right at a fragile window with no damage resulting. A player can rally in his living room against a picture window with these balls. (The author has done it, and knows this is true.)

Rallying by one's self is much better for beginners than actual play. Beginners are as a rule so inaccurate they cannot play the ball to each other to sustain a rally. All their time is spent retrieving unplayable balls. Frustration results, and not much actual practice. More importantly, against a practice wall beginners can play small shots that go and come a short distance (12–20 feet) compared to the huge court (78 feet long). A beginner can quickly achieve success on the wall, gradually expand his play by hitting a little harder and from farther away, and thus work toward the ability to use the big court.

A further advantage of practicing on a wall is the lack of pressure. When alone one can play a poor shot without feeling guilty because it didn't go nicely to one's partner so he could play too. Mistakes don't matter, and this encourages relaxation and makes for fun rather than the tension that goes with the obligation to a playing partner. One can also stop, start, rest, speed up, or shift to a different stroke whenever one wishes.

It is not asserted here that beginners should not play on the court. They should indeed play with partners, and see how they are coming along. But they should realize that this is difficult and often beyond them at first, and should not be discouraged if success is at first rare and failure, common. The practice wall is the ladder whereby they can climb to the level of full-court play and enjoy success on the way as contrasted with a lengthy period of failure.

It is a psychological fact that people love success and abhor failure. This is particularly true of children, who live very much in the present and seldom can be motivated by a promise of long-term success. They want to succeed *now*, today, at once. On the court only the more talented can do this. The majority cannot, and are turned off. On the wall everybody can do well almost immediately, each playing at his own speed and distance; but attempting what he *can* do rather than what he perhaps can't do. If the ball comes from too far, they can't judge it. If the bounce is too big, they can't handle it. Beginners need a miniature game, and the wall provides it.

Many fail to realize that the wall needn't be a dull affair. One can play forehands or backhands or serves. Or one can serve, and try to play the rebound; or play forehand to backhand to forehand—great for practice on changing grips and feet. Little games can be invented like, "I hit, you hit," or, "If I rally three in a row, I win." Parents can play with children on the wall by tapping little ones to them and encouraging them: cheering their successes and making light of their failures.

Ball machines are excellent for anyone who is intermediate or better. They are excellent for drilling a specific shot. The wall is best for beginners.

Why does one hear so little about practice walls if they are so effective? Because a big wall at a club, made of concrete or plywood measuring ten feet high and sixty feet long cannot be packaged and sold. Beyond the small rebound net, there is nothing in practice walls for the tennis industry. So the greatest teaching aid there is tends to be neglected while all others are constantly trumpeted far and wide. But think about it: A wall *is* a ball machine; it throws the ball back repeatedly. Maintenance is low. It is always there. It lasts indefinitely. A really big one (120 feet) can accommodate ten or more players, so that in a group lesson everybody is hitting all the time. For teaching and learning the mechanics of the game, it is the king of aids and should be the first priority in the budget at every club that has a program for beginners.

BEGINNERS: SECOND STAGE

As soon as a beginner can play the ball out of his hand, he wants to play the rebound off a wall or a ball that is played to him. This brings up the problem of lining up the ball. Most beginners are at a loss, have little sense of how near to get to the ball, and whiffs and wood shots are common. They need some way of measuring the proper distance to be from the ball, so they don't over- or underrun it. The head of the racket is the best yardstick. If beginners are encouraged to put the racket out to the side, with *zero* backswing, and to move until the ball is coming right to the racket head, they quickly acquire a feel for the correct proximity. They should be instructed to use the racket head like a basket: just line up the ball, catch it, and toss it back (Figures 22–23). 2020283

This contrasts sharply with what is frequently taught: point the racket at the backstop, step in, and swing. But of what avail is such a nice full swing and such nice weight transfer if it continually misses the ball? It looks fine—but there is no shot. The *first* job is to get the ball and racket together. One does not have to swing or step into the ball in order to play it. But there is no question that one must meet the ball with the strings. This is the core problem. With the racket prepared out to the side, *not* taken back, the player can at once sense, like a shortstop in baseball, that the ball is coming to his glove or it isn't, and move to adjust accordingly. With the racket pointed at the backstop the beginner may be too close, but nothing tells him he is too close. He tends to get too close because he tends to get in front of the

22

Note the total absence of backswing, footwork, weight transfer, spin. This apparently inadequate technique allows beginners to concentrate on getting the ball and racket together. It is also valuable in very advanced play when tempo is so high that there is no time for anything beyond meeting the ball.

ball so it won't get away from him. He needs to be told, "Don't get yourself in front of the ball. Get the racket head in front of it, so if you just stood there the ball would bounce off the strings. Just as it lands on your racket, toss it back." This is enough to keep him busy for a while. It is inadvisable to divert his concentration to other things such as

23

stepping in, full swing, and weight transfer, however desirable these may be. The human mind cannot concentrate simultaneously on too many things. Don't ask it to. Let the beginner focus on getting the ball and racket together, and praise him if he does it, even if footwork and balance leave much to be desired. After all, he still has plenty of worries: the slant of the face of the racket, timing, and playing the ball. Isn't that enough for now?

Talented beginners will quickly master this stage. Others will require more time. As soon as they *are* meeting the ball with the strings, then indeed they should be taught how to move better. Taking little skip steps along the base line, without crossing the feet; staying at all times in crouch, knees and waist bent; and stepping into the shot just before playing—these should now be added.

At times a talented player can learn the whole thing right at the start. Some teachers like to have a group or an individual try it without any progression (breaking it into successive steps). Then those that cannot do it are put into the progression. There is nothing wrong with this except psychologically. Most people are not that talented and start right out with a failure. It would seem preferable to put them all through the steps, allowing each to progress at his own speed as in an ungraded primary school. The talented player will swiftly reach a full-stroke status. The others will take longer but will not be asked to do more than they can handle. Psychologically it is important that they should all feel successful because people will often quit if they feel they cannot do it. "This game isn't for me." It is a good principle of teaching always to stay a trifle behind the pupil, and avoid getting way out in front of him. Push him a little, but don't hurry him. Never leave him hopelessly in the rear.

Motivation is what we constantly hear about. Too little is said about unmotivating people. Nothing is so unmotivating as discouragement. Nothing is more motivating than success. If a pupil is fed the mechanics in as small bites as possible, and allowed to chew each bite thoroughly, he will be continually motivated because he will be continually successful. If he is advanced too rapidly and flounders continually as he chokes on too large a bite, he will become discouraged, and this is a synonym for "unmotivated." One of the greatest principles in successful teaching is "teach slowly, never overteach." Possibly the greatest fault in less-experienced teachers is the impatience that leads to over-teaching. This leads to frustration both in the pupil and in the teacher, and progress is slower, not faster. This is something for every aspiring teacher to think about.

BACKSWING

This word is a troublemaker. In the first place, we do not swing back. We swing forward. We prepare the racket, move the feet, and swing forward. A definition of any ground stroke should be, "Racket ready, move your feet, play." There is no mention of backswing in this definition. None is needed.

This sounds hard to believe, but analyze what the best players do. They put the racket across—along the base line as they move toward the ball. Then, as they step into the shot, their shoulders turn so their body is sideways. This, *not* a swing of the arm, takes their racket back. Try it. Put your racket out along the base line either way, so it points at the side fence. Now turn your shoulders ninety degrees. The racket will point right at the back fence. The only swing of the arm has been to put the racket across to the forehand or backhand side. This may be done with a straight, elliptical, or circular motion. This motion is usually co-ordinated with the shoulder turn, so it *looks* as though the arm swings back one hundred eighty degrees. Actually, it swings only ninety degrees. The shoulders do half of it.

There is an additional reason why the author is a semi-fanatic in favoring a restricted backswing. Perhaps it is the most important of all. This is the factor of tempo. When the ball comes slowly, we have a lot of time. But when the ball comes quickly, we have very little time. We must not only play correctly, but we must do it literally in less than one second. How much can we swing back, then come forward and meet the ball at the optimum spot—and do it in less than a second? Obviously, a long back and forward swing, which can look so smooth and lovely, is totally impossible. The ball is passing us as we start the racket forward. We are always late, and can't seem to cure the fatal malady. A short swing is the only solution.

A LITTLE PROOF

Some may think the above is exaggerated. Figure it out—it is quite simple. Sixty miles per hour is 88 feet per second. Hard serves travel 100 miles per hour and up. This is over 145 feet per second. The court is 78 feet long. Therefore the ball, from the server's racket to the receiver's racket, covers the distance in a hair more than half a second. *And,* we need a little time to pick up the ball with our eyes to see if it is coming to the forehand or backhand. Therefore, it is no exaggeration to state that we have less than half a second in which to prepare the racket and meet the ball. It should be noted also that a hard serve is not the only time when the ball gets onto us quickly. How much time do we have when an opponent is playing crisp volleys from the net position? How much time when he attacks with a hard forehand? The better the tennis, the more constant is this factor of high tempo and the unavoidable necessity to adapt to the conditions it imposes.

There may be a further objection: This is all fine for the top players, but what connection has it with beginners, intermediates, and advanced but more average players? There are several relationships. First, it is difficult to learn with a big long swing and then cut it down as progress brings one up against better players who are more forcing. It is like starting over again. One's first move—getting the racket ready—must be drastically altered. A strong muscle habit, cultivated over time by many dutiful repetitions so it is an instant reflex must now be eliminated or sharply reduced. This is difficult, frustrating, and a tremendous waste of time. Second, it is very easy to teach or learn a very short backswing and then say, "I think when I have time I might swing a little bigger." It is easy to expand a small swing, but very hard to cut down a big swing that is habitual. Third, anyone learning the game does not know how good he will get. A teacher cannot say with any certainty, "This kid will be good—this one won't." So much depends on desire, willingness to work at it, and later physical maturity of often gangling awkward teen-agers. Stan Smith, one reads, was laughed at by his peers when he was in the all-hands-and-feet stage. As he reached physical maturity he surprised everyone by becoming a great player. It would seem advisable for everyone to learn or be taught a method that imposes no limits on progress—a method that can go as far as talent and desire make possible. The habits of the beginner should relate to future progress even though it is as yet unpredictable, and should not involve any periods of unlearning what has been learned at great pains.

MOVING WELL

This relates closely to the concept of the near-zero back-swing. Every reader is invited to try it for himself: run toward either corner, from the center, and simultaneously take a big swing. It is immediately awkward, destroys poise and balance, and reduces quickness. By contrast, put the racket along the base line and run to the same spot. At once poise and balance return and quickness is enhanced. When they run, the best players have a *quiet* racket (out to the side and almost motionless) and very quick feet.

Why is this true? Because the motion of the big back-swing opposes (pulls against) the effort of the legs to get us there. We are fighting ourselves, as in an isometric conditioning exercise. One force cancels out a good part of the other, so the net result is small after a great effort. The opposing forces also destroy all feeling of balance and poise. We literally tend to tear ourselves apart instead of keeping ourselves in one neat balanced package as we move.

Additionally, if we take a big swing, it may be that we get within reach of the ball, but what does the "we" mean? It means our body and legs are there, but the racket is way back, far from the ball. On a tough "get" we cannot bring the racket forward to the ball quickly enough, or must do it so frantically that control is impaired or destroyed. How many times have we all heard a player rage, "Why do I get there and then *miss* it?" Almost always the answer is, "Too much swing on the run."

Moving well, rather than just moving, is a distinction we all notice in great players like Rosewall, who moves superbly. One of the great secrets is to take small steps. Many players strain mightily toward the ball, but take large strides, lose poise, appear awkward. They seem to go "galumph, galumph" where Rosewall goes lightly, "step, step, step" in rapid succession, so his feet are constantly under him, not straddled out, and he arrives perfectly poised and able to make a fine shot even at high tempo. Surely most of us do not have his talent, but equally surely we can realize our best level of play by imitating his method: a lot of quick small steps rather than a few big ones. This can be practiced quite easily by just doing it. Put the racket to the side and, keeping it quiet, move in a crouch to the corner with a quick succession of small steps. Moving well can be learned just as racket skill can be learned, and as tempo rises with better play, moving well becomes increasingly important: You can't make the stroke you have learned if you can't get there in balance.

II

Ground Strokes for Intermediates

An intermediate can keep the ball in play, but now he aspires to do a little more than that. He should strive for better depth, trying to make all his strokes land behind the service line or deeper. He should feel that he can now play an opponent's weakness by aiming all shots to a single half of the court. He may even try for an accurate attacking shot on fat chances, aiming on such occasions fairly close to either side line. Above all he will feel, "I can get it in if I play gently. I'd like to hit it harder, but when I do it goes out." To implement these tactics and, in particular, to achieve greater pace without loss of consistency, he must now learn to stroke the ball, i.e., to spin it.

TOPSPIN

Every base-line shot must go *up* from the racket in order to clear the net. This is 100 per cent true. That means there are no exceptions. Even a high ball (shoulder high or above) is only two or three feet above the net. From forty feet back from the net—the normal base-line position—the very slightest angle down, aided by gravity, will play into the net. Therefore, with absolutely no exceptions the ball must leave the racket going up.

If we play it up, and hit it gently, gravity will pull it into the court after it crosses the net. If we hit hard, gravity may do it and it may not. Many balls will fly past the whole court before gravity pulls them down. We need additional control. We achieve it by using topspin.

THE SIGNIFICANCE OF SPIN

When a ball spins as it flies through the air, one side of the ball is turning toward the oncoming air; the other away from the air stream. There is more air pressure on the side that opposes the flow of the passing air. The ball is pushed by this pressure, so its flight becomes a curve. Topspin means that the top of the ball is moving toward the oncoming air; the bottom of the ball backward away from the air stream. There is more pressure on the top of the ball than on the bottom, so the ball curves down. Thus, it is possible to hit a ball very hard, hit it up so it clears the net by a good safe margin, and still have it arc down and strike the court before it goes out.

Have you ever wondered why a baseball player is said to "hit" the ball, while a tennis player is said to "stroke" the ball? Spin is the difference. A baseball player does not really care how far the ball goes. He does not worry about the length of his shot. If it goes over everything in sight, he has that most desirable of hits, a home run. A tennis player must, no matter how hard he hits, make sure the ball comes down inside the lines. Therefore he "strokes" the ball. That is, he wipes it so it rotates in such a way as to make it behave as he wishes. Control of length is absent in baseball; ever present in tennis.

The bounce of a tennis ball is also affected sharply by the spin it carries. Topspin will jump forward and up. Sidespin will kick sideways. Backspin on a ball with any pace will skid low. Gentle backspin will stop dead and bounce straight up. That's why it is desirable on a drop shot, since it makes the ball stay right where it lands just beyond the net.

Combinations produce combined results. A twist service with side and top (diagonal) spin will bounce high and out to the side toward which it spins. A sliced approach shot will skid low and out to the side toward which the front of the ball is turning. The amount of "kick" (the variation from a normal bounce) will vary with the receptivity of the court surface to spin. On some the spin will "take" with marked results, on others (smoother) the ball tends to skid straight no matter how it is played because there is little "grab" to the surface. Grass is a skiddy surface. Clay is a grabby surface. Hard and synthetic courts vary according to the finish.

On any surface the flight of the ball through the air can and must be controlled by spin whenever the ball is played vigorously enough so that gravity will not do the job. That is why topspin should be the first new skill acquired by an intermediate.

Incidentally, this line between beginner and intermediate is entirely arbitrary. Someone else may choose to say that this is advanced, that our "beginner, second stage" was intermediate. There is no point in arguing about these divisions. The only important point is to get a clear grasp of the stages through which one must progress in order to reach the goal, which is competent advanced play. It matters little whether we have special words for the various stages, or which stages are included in the meaning of each successive word. Some like numerous divisions—beginner, middle beginner, advanced beginner, lower intermediate, intermediate, upper intermediate, etc. This is all personal choice. But that there are levels of skill and that there can and should be logical progression from one to the next is difficult to refute, in both tactics and technique. It is the progression that counts, not the nomenclature.

THE CORE OF RACKET SKILLS

The basic truths about racket technique are very simple. The racket meets the ball and one of three things must happen: the racket goes "through" the ball (playing "flat"); the top edge of the racket leads off the ball (always topspin); or the bottom edge of the racket leads off the ball (every cut shot). Since flat hitting gives no spin, we discard it as useless, except perhaps when killing a short lob when no spin is needed—we just slam the ball. Actually, playing flat is not a stroke. It is a hit. There is no wiping or stroking effect, so how can we call it a stroke?

This leaves two techniques, topspin and cut, and every shot is one or the other. What is a slice service except a gigantic chop or cut shot? A drop shot is a tiny feathery cut shot. A topspin lob is exactly the same thing as a topspin drive: We play the ball up and spin it forward, but we enormously increase the amount of up and the amount of forward spin. An angled passing shot is again just a topspin drive with less weight (for less length) and sharper spin so the ball will drop immediately, very short, as soon as it crosses the net. A volley is an abbreviated stiff-wristed cut shot. A slice with a lot of "side" is a cut shot: We cut from the outside in. A chop means we cut from above down. Undercut means we cut the bottom of the ball, as in a backspin lob. Thus, every shot is a variation on one of the two themes, top or cut, leading off the ball with the top or bottom edge of the racket.

In passing it would be well to scotch another tennis myth, "It is bad to cut the ball." There are more cut shots than topspin shots. To play tennis without being able to cut is like trying to walk with one leg. You can't get along without the other. Then why do people say this? It merely means that if all you can do is cut the ball, then you are limited. You don't have any good hard drives, for which topspin is necessary. But if you can only topspin, then you can't volley, serve, drop shot, slice approach, block lob, chip return, or dig up a low ball you can barely reach. Enough said? Topspin and cut are *both* indispensable techniques, and it is pointless to compare them as though one had a choice. You can't volley well with topspin, and you can't drive well without it.

WEIGHT

There is another aspect of core technique: getting the weight into the ball. For the most part, the racket does not make the ball go. The racket spins the ball; the weight makes it go. While this is not totally true, it is substantially true and more so than many think. Who has not slipped or been caught off balance so it is impossible to achieve any weight transfer? What happens? The racket plays the ball without any drive from the legs (which is how we use our weight) and a surprisingly feeble shot always results. A person with a strong wrist may snap the racket and get pretty good pace, but this is, of course, very difficult to control. No good player does this by choice: He prefers to use his weight, thus getting a smooth controlled shot rather than a reckless snap.

Thus, to make a good stroke, a player must stroke the ball with the strings and simultaneously apply pressure with the weight. This is what is meant by the old cliché, "hit through the ball." It does *not* mean hit through it with the racket (the racket wipes and goes *off* the ball on the follow-through). It means that whether the racket is going high to low (service or chop) from the outside in (sidespin) or low to high (topspin) the weight *always* goes right with the shot and not anywhere else. This has a dual effect. It accelerates the ball, giving pace, and it keeps the racket on the ball longer, giving more stroke; therefore, more control. It is quite possible to spin the ball perfectly yet achieve only a puffy paceless spinny shot with no guts: that is, no weight. Therefore, it is important, whenever learning or teaching "stroke the ball with the racket," to emphasize, "Press forward as you work on the ball with the strings. Don't just spin it. Spin it *and* press it at the same time. Stay with it."

This is a composite thought: two things at once. That is why many think it should not be taught to beginners but should wait until they have achieved at least minimum skill with basic grips, preparation, timing, and meeting the ball. To expect a beginner to learn those things *plus* these concepts of stroking is asking too much. Confusion and frustration may easily result. We return again to that all-important injunction, "Don't bite off more than you can chew."

TECHNICAL SUMMARY

If a player can learn both to spin the ball forward and backward while simultaneously applying his weight, he has laid the foundation for every shot in the game. Building this foundation is, in this book, the objective in the stage here termed "intermediate." Once these skills are acquired (and not before) a player can move on to what we call "advanced" tennis, which means the specific and refined application of these principles to tactical situations.

INTERMEDIATES AND SPIN: TOPSPIN FIRST

Intermediates should not initially be confused with too much theoretical chatter about all the variations of cut and topspin. They wish to play their drives with more authority. They need, first, to master moderate topspin. The rest is better left unsaid. Let them concentrate on this one concept until they get the hang of it: wipe up and press forward. They will learn it faster and will not be diverted or mixed up by other worries.

If the ball is to go up we must play the middle of the back of the ball or even a hair below the middle. If the racket comes from behind and below the ball, contacts this spot on the ball, and wipes it up, the ball will both go up and rotate forward. It is a good idea to do it gently at first, preferably against a practice wall which keeps returning the ball. If a player will do it slowly and thoughtfully until he gets the feel of wiping and pressing, he can easily speed it up, enlarge his swing, and whale away. It is a fact that most people want to try a "good one" instantly, before they even know what it is they are attempting. One learns much more quickly by gentle experimentation and trial and error, with no thought of power until some skill and feel have been attained. Then do it a little faster, a little bigger. The speed will come; the skill is what must be worked on (Figures 24–26).

It also brings quicker results to do one thing at a time. Learn a topspin forehand, and forget the backhand. Then concentrate exclusively on the backhand. A very good method for achieving the desired concentration on one objective is to make a rule: "Every time I play a ball out of my hand, even if only to send a ball over to my opponent so he can serve again, I'll toss it up, let it bounce, and send him a topspin forehand." It is quite surprising how many times we do this—to start a rally if merely hitting with someone, or to give him the ball when it is his service. If we regularly carefully practice the skill we are seeking to develop, this method means we will keep eternally coming back to it. After the forehand is going pretty well (after some weeks or more?) and we decide, "Now I'm going to learn a topspin backhand," switch: Play every loose ball with a *careful* topspin backhand. This keeps our mind on it and keeps our muscles constantly repeating it. It really speeds the learning process; often by 50 per cent or more.

24

Topspin: Basic Drive

Details: Racket goes from low to high, higher than in previous illustrations (Catch and Toss, Figures 22, 23). The ball will roll down the racket, or the racket will wipe up the back of the ball. This is a basic deep drive—note the slightly open face. Contrast with Figure 35, Base-line Passing Shot, which shows a more closed face.

25

26

INTERMEDIATES: SLICE SECOND

Once an intermediate can make fairly decent topspin drives with both forehand and backhand, it is customary to regard him as "advanced." But if our analysis of basic technical needs is sound, he has only done half the job. He should learn to chop and slice. Obviously, he needs this for the execution of shots he wishes to learn as an advanced player, such as chip service return, slice approach, drop shot, underspin lob. Less obviously, he needs it for defensive purposes. If a gang of kids learn only solid topspin drive and play with each other, it is astonishing how baffled they are when they first encounter that much-maligned type known as a "chop artist." Every bounce surprises and confuses them, their timing is destroyed, and they often lose to a player who, in the warm-up, looks quite inferior. If they learn to cut and practice it against each other, they learn to handle it, to know what the bounce will do, and how best to adapt to it. In advanced play there are many top players who, in a base-line exchange, will slice their backhand viciously with great steadiness.

The intermediate stage is not too soon to begin teaching both execution of and adaption to this useful and prevalent technique.

In learning slice or how to cut the ball a sense of humor is a great help. Players accustomed to using topspin have developed a habit of coming from below the ball and following through high. When they do this and cut the ball, it pops right up and goes far out. They must learn that in a topspin shot the ball rolls down the racket and goes lower than the follow-through, while in a cut shot the ball rolls up the racket and goes higher than the follow-through. All of a sudden they must swing more from high to low rather than low to high. Inevitably the adjustment is difficult and many crazy shots precede a controlled slice.

Another obstacle is the myth that to cut means to go under the ball. This is the converse of the myth that to topspin means to hit the top of the ball. Of course, if one cuts under the bottom of the ball it sails right up into the air, fifteen or twenty feet over the net, sometimes almost over the backstop. Players must learn that just as with topspin we play the *back* of the ball to get a reasonably level flight, slightly up to clear the net, but nothing like what happens if we really go under it.

Even after they learn to "keep it down" the ball still sails past the base line. Why? Because there is now no topspin on it to keep it in. They must learn that a slice is not a back-and-forth swing like a topspin, but is, to a major extent, a crossing motion from the outside in. The racket must approach the ball from the outside, not from directly behind it. By drawing or pulling across it, the racket does not go forward as much with the ball as with an ordinary topspin stroke, so the ball gets less speed, and gravity will keep it in. A vicious slice *spins* fast; it doesn't *go* fast. If it goes fast, it will indeed tend to sail out even if played reasonably low over the net. The slice not only fails to arc it into the court, it actually tends to hold it up against gravity, so if given speed it will plane and hang up until it has gone too far— and is out.

A good slice is a pull with the racket, drawing the strings across the back of the ball, plus a push with the weight (Figures 27–29). These two motions are almost at right an-

27

Slicing a Backhand

Note the crossing nature of the swing—from far out to the left (Figure 27), to far over to the right (Figure 29). Then note the movement of the weight: straight forward behind the shot. These simultaneous moves are almost at right angles to each other. The racket moves from the outside in, the weight, from back to front. The racket spins the ball. Weight controls both pace and length. The shot shown is a sliced approach: In Figure 29 the player is advancing even as he finishes the shot. Note the left foot here has walked through.

gles to each other. This concept, when new to a player, is strange and wonderful, almost unbelievable. To prepare the racket out to the side, diagonally out and back rather than directly back, is very tough at first. It all seems very queer.

28

29

But learning to cross off the ball as contrasted with going forward with it is the basic technique necessary to control the length of a cut ball.

It is more obvious on a chop. Here the racket prepares above the ball and cuts right down the back of it, finishing low. The ball, however, since it rolls up the racket, goes roughly horizontally out from the racket. Now think of chopping sideways on a lower ball, chopping horizontally from left to right (backhand), or right to left (forehand). This is a slice. Think of a slice service: It is a huge chop. Now think of serving a ball from knee height instead of from over the head. The chopping motion must now be almost horizontal, from right to left, in order to get it over the net. (Of course there is another difference. We use wrist on the service but not on a sliced ground stroke, but that is irrelevant to the point being made.)

This concept of crossing the ball, and of two motions (racket and weight) that are almost at right angles to each other, is belabored at length here just because it is not generally perceived, understood, or taught. But watch a fine player like Billie Jean King make a sliced approach. Do not watch the ball leave her racket. Watch her racket leave the ball. You will see the racket go to the right. You will see her right elbow go way out to the right as she pulls across the ball. (And Billie Jean has a very good slice approach shot.)

One common misunderstanding must be avoided. The weight does not go across. It goes directly forward in the direction of the shot: straight behind the ball. Billie Jean gets great accuracy because she keeps her weight moving exactly with the shot all the way through, even though her arm and racket go to the right (on a backhand), off the ball, not with it. This not only makes the spinning shot have pace, be accurate, and take a nasty low bounce, it also gives her a good start toward the net.

In clarifying one's thinking about this business of the racket going one way and the weight another, a different approach can be taken. It is the racket *leaving* the ball that creates spin.

Coming to the ball does not create spin. To create topspin the racket must go up, allowing the ball to roll down in a brushing action. It is the racket going briskly up and off the back of the ball that engenders the forward spin on the ball. (Here is that near right angle again: The racket goes up, the weight goes straight.) To create slice or sidespin the racket must cross the back of the ball and go off it briskly so the ball is set to turning while it is on the racket. If by contrast the racket goes right with the ball and not off the ball, no spin is created. A "flat" shot results. This is why all topspin follow-throughs consist of a very high flourish, slice follow-throughs go from the outside in and across to the other side, chop follow-throughs go from high to very low—the service being an easy example to visualize. In *every* case the racket goes off the ball, not with it, while the weight "hits through the ball" every time. Understanding this is the basis for understanding how to stroke rather than hit, and to stroke is the means to control—it is what we call "technique."

So intermediates should be introduced to chopping and slicing. After they have become familiar with it and begin to hit the court more often than the backstop, a very good exercise is to have them topspin a shot, then slice the next, then topspin, then slice, etc. This is an excellent drill to establish clearly in their minds and in their *feel* the opposite nature of the two skills: Lift up on the topspin, hold the slice down; prepare somewhat below for the topspin, somewhat above for the slice; follow-through high for topspin, low for slice; go forward with the ball when topspinning, pull across it when slicing. Anyone can drill on a practice wall: Practice one skill until good at it, then try shifting as described above. It is fun and leads to a balanced technical foundation.

III

Advanced Ground Strokes:
The Base-line Exchange

The tactical instructions given in preceding sections to beginners and intermediates are extremely limited. After all, of what use are a lot of cagey concepts if one cannot execute them accurately? A top intermediate has mastered technique in the rough. He can topspin his drives and get them in reasonably firmly. He can exchange slices fairly steadily. He is now prepared for the greatest fun in tennis: He is ready to develop a real game as contrasted with being "pretty tough" but not having any specific polished shots or tactical plans. In sum, the lid on tactics is off.

This does not mean he will suddenly become great. It does mean he is ready to apply his technique to specific match-play situations. He is ready to learn the concept of percentages as applied all over the court, and this is a very big job. There are many match situations that recur constantly. Service and net play are not the subjects of this book, and are therefore omitted. But included here are the base-line rally, defensive play when an opponent is at net, approach shots, drop shots, lobs, deception, combinations of contrasting shots, and that all-important play, the return of service. Mastering all this will keep an intermediate busy for a while!

We are now relating technique to tactical objectives, and tactics dictate technique, not vice versa. Here is a brief summary of some basic points.

Base-line exchange: Hit cross-court or hit everything to one side; i.e., play a weakness. Stress steadiness and depth.

Base-line defense: Use both straight and cross-court, extra topspin, the lob, deception.

Return of service: Take it early, play cross-court, learn to topspin, be aggressive, be ingenious.

Approach shots: Play straight, go up to net wide, practice approaches as a separate technique.

Drop shot: Technique and deception are essential; relate it to approach shots.

Match play: Be adaptable, find a way.

THE BASE-LINE EXCHANGE

A few years ago all "big" tournaments were played on grass or hard courts. All these courts favored the offense; so much so that anyone who didn't follow his service to net was, as a rule, not a contender in top play. Therefore, there usually was no such thing as a base-line rally in men's tennis. One player or the other was always at net. (Women played back a lot but did not receive the attention they get at present.)

Today this is changed. Recognizing that tennis, however popular, was a lopsided game, leading clubs such as Forest Hills and the Longwood Cricket Club installed slower, softer surfaces on which the defense and offense are better balanced. It is still desirable to get to the net, but one must be far more careful in one's choice of the instant to attack. The baseliner has a little more time and will successfully repulse any ill-considered foray into the forecourt. Therefore, there are now frequent base-line rallies as each contestant maneuvers and waits for a chance to attack with a good probability of coming out on top. It is no longer a simple game.

The possibilities open to a player at the base line are quite limited. He cannot win the point. He is too far away to put the ball past his opponent because the ball has too far to travel to get past him. The other fellow always has time to get it. Therefore, striking out for winners is non-percentage and leads only to more errors than aces. He cannot put the ball very far away from his opponent: The court is too long and narrow. He must wait for the short ball that allows him to move in where more can be done with less risk and greater promise of reward. During this sparring match he has two defensive responsibilities and two offensive choices.

Defensively he must be steady: Never give the point away through an error. This means he should avoid aiming close to the lines. He should aim for rather large areas so even if his aim is not perfect, his allowance for error in height, direction, and length will still keep the ball in the court. This may seem overconservative but it isn't. He *can't* win the point, so what profit is there in taking a high risk? To do so is like buying a stock that can't go up but may well go down. It is non-percentage. This is a very important truth that is often hard to learn for fiery, idealistic young comers who are out to do something impressive every time they play the ball. They must learn that one cannot rush in where angels fear to tread, that one *must* have reasonable patience, keep the ball in play, and attack selectively rather than all the time. Don't we all know players—pretty good ones—who are known as "big missers"? They have not yet learned this base-line fundamental: Be steady and "wait your opponent out."

The second defensive necessity is depth. If one's ball is landing consistently halfway or more from the service line to the base line it is very difficult for an opponent to move in advantageously. One has the advantage of a boxer with a long reach who constantly keeps his left jab way out there so his opponent can't get close enough to deal a telling blow. In order to get depth it is necessary to play comparatively high over the net. Even a hard hit ball from the base line should clear the net by two to three feet so it will go deep. This is so important that one may almost distinguish between base-line errors: If a player hits too deep, over the base line, that is a good error, at least he was trying for depth. If he hits the net, that is a bad error because even if it had just sneaked over, it would have been a short ball inviting a successful attack by his opponent. A player should *never* hit the net in a base-line rally because he shouldn't be playing anywhere near it.

Thus, the defensive responsibilities of the baseliner can be summed up by establishing two negative ideals: Never lose the point and never give your opponent a chance to win the point.

What can a baseliner do offensively? First, he can analyze his opponent and if the opponent is weaker on one side, it is a good policy to play just about every ball to that side. This is the well known and obvious rule, "Always play a weakness." It spite of its being so obvious, many players don't know how to do it. They play one or two balls to the weakness, then try to run the opponent by playing the other side.

Back he comes with his strongest shot and perhaps takes charge from there on.

Playing a weakness means to forget all about running the opponent; just pound the soft spot. If a poor return lets you move in, pound it there again (even if he is standing there!) and follow to the net. If the volley or overhead can't be put away, put it to the weakness until one comes back that can be a winner to the strong side. The idea is that insofar as it is within your capabilities your opponent will *never* get to hit his strong shot—not even once.

Sometimes this absolutely rigid method must be modified. A player with a big forehand and a weak backhand will continually run around the ball and frustrate attempts to play his backhand. Then it is necessary at times to play a ball wide to his strength so as to open up the weakness and "keep him honest." This should be done as infrequently as will achieve the purpose. The ideal is still to pound the weakness every possible time.

Most good players are not so unbalanced in their skills. They do not have one very good side and one very bad side. They are more nearly even. Many will have a forceful but somewhat erratic forehand plus a rather harmless but very steady backhand. There is no particular reason to be obvious and play every ball to one spot. What constitutes good tactics in this very common situation and many others like it?

The answer is to play every ball cross-court. This is in direct contradiction to what many think; namely, that one should "move an opponent around" by playing first to one side, then the other. But the reasons favoring constant cross-court play are very compelling. It is a safer shot because it goes over the low part of the net. It is safer because it goes on the long diagonal. There is less chance of hitting out. It is safer because it is aimed at the whole court instead of a narrow strip down one side. It is stronger defensively because it gives an opponent little chance to run you: He *must* play parallel to you (straight) or hit it back to you (cross-court). By contrast, if you play straight, he can angle cross-court away from you, running you a much greater distance. Thus, it fulfills all our defensive requirements by encouraging steadiness and avoiding giving the opponent an opening. It is also stronger offensively because a cross-court goes more away from an opponent, while a straight shot goes parallel to him. If two players rally, one hitting everything straight and the other playing constantly cross-court, the straight hitter will run two or three times as much as the cross-court player. Try it on the court yourself. It is a fact.

Thus the cross-court is easier, safer, stronger defensively and offensively. Some may think this is too forceful a presentation—too absolute. Think again: Who is the most outstanding baseliner today? Chris Evert. What does she do? She hits just about *every* ball cross-court and she does it well—and she always wins out from the base line. Her few losses are to net players like Billie Jean King—not to baseliners. The proof of the pudding is in the eating—and there you are. Chris has practiced cross-courts until she is very good at making them. It is very difficult to out-cross-court her. But if her opponent plays straight, Chris just plays her other cross-court and runs the opponent hard. She wins both ways.

FIGHT AND CONCENTRATION

We hear a great deal about concentration, the killer instinct, determination, consistency, and so forth. Some players concentrate so hard they have a horrible scowl on their faces throughout the play. This may all be very good stuff (though one may be permitted to suggest it is often overdone). But the greatest factor in consistent fight is to *know what you are doing*. If one player knows what he is going to do in a given situation and has practiced it until he is good at it, he is all set before he takes the court. He knows before he goes out there that if the ball comes to his backhand, he will play cross-court. He has no worries, no doubts, no misgivings, no constant problem of decision making. By contrast a player without a plan takes the court and must decide *very* quickly where he is going to place each ball. Surely he will make some bad decisions. Surely he will attempt some non-percentage shots and make a few needless errors. It is inevitable. How can a player like this ever hope to be as tough as Chris Evert? All we hear about is Chris Evert's great strokes. People should give her more credit for the rocklike soundness of her tactics. Her thinking is as sound as her execution, and is too seldom recognized as a major factor in her unequalled record on the base line.

Once a player has gone through the stages of learning how to play the ball—what might be called the technical stage—then he should, first of all, perfect his cross-court drives until they are solid, deep, and very consistent. With this skill he will begin to win the rally (not the point) more often than his opponent. He will get short returns that offer him a good chance to attack.

ACHIEVING DEPTH

In refining base-line strokes the greatest problem frequently is depth. This can be called the "third aim." We must, obviously, aim straight (not to the left or right). We must, obviously, aim at the right height (not too low or high). The third aim concerns length (not too short or too long), and it comes almost entirely from the legs.

It is a good idea to experiment a little. Put topspin on a ball and, as you do it, try to feel that while you are wiping it you are pressing it or carrying it a certain distance by shoving with your back leg. Soon you will feel how far it will carry before the topspin takes hold and arcs it down. You can carry it only a little, and with the *same* height and spin it will drop very short (desirable for an angled passing shot). Or you can carry it long so it goes past the service line and then breaks down for a very deep shot. In other words, if one consciously gets set to push with the back leg, one develops what can be termed a telescopic feeling for length. Like an accordion it can be opened up a little or a lot, enabling one to play short for an angle or a net-player's feet, or long for good depth in a base-line rally.

Here is where footwork and balance, as distinguished from racket skill, become very important. To drive something—in this case a ball—means to get behind it and shove. We must bend the knees in preparation, then shove by straightening the legs: pushing against the ground. If we are always crouched in getting ready, we can use as much or as little of the potential shove as we choose. This is often referred to as "weight transfer," since we push off the back foot and go over the front foot. But basically this means that we don't merely advance one foot or position ourselves sideways. We actually get set to push with our legs, and then we do push. This shove is what gives us length and controls the amount of length. It must be varied: If a very deep shot forces us back six or eight feet behind the base line, we must carry the ball both higher and farther to get good depth on the return. By contrast, if we are running in to get a drop volley and wish to tweak a cross-court passing shot, we probably don't push at all when we play: We want the ball to go up over the net and at once drop down again. If there is any leg drive, it must be minimal or the ball will go too far and land in the alley. These are the two extremes.

Many players do not have a good sense of length. When forced back deep behind the base line they make their usual shot. It lands inside the service line rather than well behind it, and their opponent can attack at once. Then from within the base line they will use the same length and hit out.

If a player is giving a good shove and spinning the ball well and it still keeps landing short, he is probably playing too low over the net. One tennis myth is the belief that low net skimmers are the best shots. This is often not true. Playing low results in increased errors in the net, and many of those that do go over land short and invite attack. If one plays very hard, of course the shot must be lower, but the average solid base-line shot usually needs to be about a yard above the net if it is to achieve good depth.

Playing in the wind necessitates constant switching—from extra push against the wind to a careful restraint when you change sides and the wind tends to carry the ball over the base line. It is not possible to say, "Play the ball like this and you'll be all set under any conditions." Position on the court, wind, slower or faster balls, and courts—all these factors make it necessary for a player to be able to adapt. Even in the course of a set the balls may get lighter or heavier: One must feel the need for greater or lesser push to control length. The ability to adapt technique to actual match circumstances is a factor that needs special attention by anyone hoping to achieve excellence. In a wind, it does no good to moan, "How can anyone play when it's like this?" It's blowing just as hard for the opponent too, and after you finish your complaint it keeps right on blowing. Adapt, or lose out.

If a player is very strong, he can lower his shot a bit (to about two feet over the net) and use his strength to force his opponent in the rally. He must experiment to see how hard he can play without becoming a big misser. Players that are of less than average strength, and this includes many women, should play higher (about four to six feet) over the net in order to achieve depth. Never mind what somebody else does. Figure out how you, with your strength, can achieve consistent depth without continually straining to hit harder and lower. It must be comfortable or you cannot sustain it through a match.

Years ago when Bobby Riggs was one of the world's great players, he frequently played six to ten feet above the net in a base-line rally. He drove his opponents mad. His ball was always a few feet from the base line. They couldn't get in on him, and they couldn't outsteady him. His consistent depth was phenomenal. Once three all-time greats (I think it was Kramer, Budge, and Gonzalez) were asked, "Who was the most underrated player you ever knew?" They answered in chorus, "Bobby Riggs." Riggs did not usually hit really hard, but his mastery of depth made him a thorn in the side of even the greatest of the big hitters. Of course, if an opponent came to net, he *could* hit much lower with his passing shots (which were tops), but as a small fellow playing bigger men, he never tired himself by attempting to outdo them at big hitting. He stayed right with them by playing higher. This is something the average athlete, talented but not supertalented, might do well to imitate. If that little guy Riggs can do so well, why can't some of the rest of us? One of the greatest aspects of tennis is the fact that any decent athlete, *if* he knows himself and stays within himself, can play the game very effectively. To be a world champion, yes, you must have the talent. But to be a good player is within the reach of many, many thousands.

The famous Riggs "moon ball" drive is one way to vary base-line play. Another is to change spins. The greatest artist at this ploy was undoubtedly Bill Tilden. By now he is a legend and is endowed with superhuman talents. He was not superhuman. Due to his reputation, everyone who played him was always "up." Many times his opponent would start out red hot, playing over his head, and would take the first set. But Tilden was perhaps the most versatile player who ever lived. He would change his game like a chameleon, shift from solid drives to vicious slices, heavy topspin loops, and many changes of speed. It was amazing to watch him pull his opponent down out of the clouds and eventually destroy him. The different speeds and the mean kick bounces would bother his opponent, break up his perfect timing, knock him out of his early perfect groove, and undermine his confidence. He would gradually falter, have more and more trouble, and finally end in frustration. It was laughable to read the uneducated comments of some of the less-knowledgeable reporters. "He was beating the great Tilden, but unaccountably he let up after the first set and Big Bill took over." Allison Danzig of the New York *Times* did Tilden's genius full justice. Most others didn't realize what went on and couldn't understand why Tilden won so consistently, even after a bad start.

We can't all be Tildens. We can, however, develop the ability to shift from hard drives to higher softer drives or continual slicing when we encounter an opponent stronger than we are at the base line. We all know the old cliché, "Always change a losing game." But how do you change if you can only play the ball one way? If that won't work, all you can do is lose. Tilden was once described as having seven backhands. He was the Toscanini of tennis. All that is suggested here is that we should develop two backhands: a topspin and a slice. With this equipment, we all can be quite versatile: We can try the topspin, try the slice, try rushing the net at every chance, try pulling our opponent into the net. Thus, we have four shots at finding a way to win. That's pretty good versatility even if it does leave out Tilden's great stage presence and showmanship and his extra variations in using spin. It is an objective that is not beyond the capabilities of any average athlete willing to work at it.

HOW TO PRACTICE

Most players go out and hit a lot, but they hit everything—forehands, backhands, some net play, etc. This is not a good policy. It is much more profitable to concentrate on one shot. Find someone else who wants to improve, and use drills that center on one specific skill. These drills can be games such as:

1. Trade topspin backhands cross-court. The target is half the court. Whoever puts the ball in the forehand court loses the point.

2. Trade topspin backhands and make it tougher. The target is one quarter of the court. The ball must land on the backhand side behind the service line. This is a good depth drill.

3. Play the same two games with sliced backhands. Practice of this kind is fun—it's a game—and it makes you really try: Every time you fail to achieve the objective, you lose. These drills or games are great "tougheners." They build that consistency that is so impressive in Chris Evert and is so lacking in many "good looking" players.

GRIPS AGAIN

Some players like to vary their grips just a trifle in switching from forward to backspin. If a tiny shift makes things go better, don't think it is wrong. It is right, and no one should shrink from it. After a bit you won't even know you do it—it becomes an unconscious habit. A tiny shift (roughly, one eighth inch) toward the continental from an eastern grip often makes it easier to get a heavy slice. The test is, do you feel ready to do what you plan? If, when you topspin, the racket keeps trying to go under the ball a bit, this is a sure indication that you are trying to topspin with a slice grip. Don't fight the natural motions of your arm and body. Use that grip for slice, but get a trifle more on top of (behind) the racket for the topspin shot. It is very difficult to make your arm, hand, and wrist do what they don't want to do. It is perfectly simple to change the racket any way you choose.

It should be cautioned, however, that the results of a grip change are surprisingly drastic. Even a small change can make the ball go decisively higher or lower. Therefore if you experiment with changes, make them *very* small. A little bit goes a long way. But just because a little means such a lot, it is important to experiment if you are one of these players who can slice but "just can't topspin," or vice versa. A slight change can often make quite easy what formerly seemed nearly impossible. This is particularly true on backhands. Many, many players can slice but have no luck with topspin. The grip is almost always the reason: They are too continental. They should not discard that grip. A steady slice is a valuable shot. They should *add* the ability to close the face a little by shifting to an eastern—then they will find it comparatively easy to learn topspin. The ball will go in the net at first because they are not accustomed to the more closed face and do not allow for it. They just have to get used to that and learn to aim higher. The strangeness and uncertainty are soon overcome by persistence.

Once again, at the risk of overdoing it, stress is placed on having an open mind and having no fear of trying something new. Most players are incredibly conservative. They try something once, with great misgiving, then say "I can't do that. It feels funny." Of course it feels funny. Anything you are not used to will feel "funny"—i.e., strange. If you had always walked on your hands, it would feel very strange to walk on your feet—but *after* you got used to it, you'd like it much better. The test is not how it feels the first time, but does it make sense? If it makes sense, do it enough to get used to it before making a final judgment that may permanently limit your chances of adding to your resources. One of the most difficult aspects of teaching is not what to teach, but to overcome most people's unwillingness to try something a little different from whatever they have always done. Such stubborn reluctance is understandable but not desirable.

It helps to discard the word "change." If you have a good slice, no one should change it. The idea is to acquire an additional resource, not to throw your game away and start over again. It is not a matter of losing anything you already have developed at great pains. It is a matter of learning a new skill that will increase both your enjoyment and your effectiveness. A new skill may bug you a little at first before you get the feel of it, but if you persist through this learning stage, it will become a new plaything as well as a new resource. The game is more fun, and you are a better player.

IV

Return of Service

In all base-line play, return of service is the most important. Any consideration of this area of the game should involve a close interweaving of tactical and technical considerations. What has perhaps been neglected in tennis literature is the fact that different tactics require different techniques: different backswing, different slants of the racket face, different grips. There are various tactics employed by the server, each of which limits the options of the receiver. But he does indeed have options, and these should be explored.

The most simple situation occurs when the server remains at the base line and does not follow in to net. In such a case, the receiver should take his time and apply regular base-line rally tactics and technique. Play a weakness or play cross-court. If the server angles the ball, the receiver should close and take the ball as early as possible to avoid being carried far out of court by the bounce. Otherwise there is no point in taking the additional risks involved in taking the ball very quickly on the rise.

There is, however, one basic that applies to every return of service: Always step forward into the ball. To play a forehand return, step *in* with the left foot—never step back with the right foot. For a backhand, step in with the right foot, never back with the left. Serving and returning can be characterized as a shoving contest. The server hopes to put on the pressure and shove the receiver back on his heels so his return will be weak and fluttery. The receiver must push back. He must give as good as he gets, or he is at once in trouble. He must be belligerent, not retiring.

This is true of any shot—we should move into the ball—but it needs particular stress in this situation because the receiver tends to feel defensive, and this tends to make him back up instead of move forward as he plays. It helps if one thinks of what one is trying to do: *Break* serve. To "break" is certainly not a passive defensive concept. It is an aggressive positive concept. It helps if one thinks, "He is trying to push me around. I'm going to push right back." If the receiver stands just behind the base line (toes against it) and steps forward into the court to play, and makes this a habit, he will find his returns (without changing his stroke in any way) will become firmer and will go deeper. Also, control improves because the moving weight keeps the racket longer on the ball.

Another helpful concept is to develop a mental image: "If the ball comes to my forehand, I'm going to move diagonally forward to the right. If to my backhand, I'm going to move diagonally forward to the left." Do not have an image of going sideways to the forehand and sideways to the backhand. Some players even go sideways and a little back each way—this is very poor since it usually produces a floater, because little if any weight gets into the return. The racket work may be perfect, but the shot is feeble. The receiver must oppose the server's weight with his own weight. This is fundamental number one in returning service.

If the server angles, the forward-move must be decisively increased. The ball is bouncing out across the alley, and if the receiver takes it late, he will be carried hopelessly out of

position for the next shot. He therefore should move sharply
forward, take the ball as soon as he possibly can, and play
back cross-court. If he can get it back rather sharply cross-
court, the server has much less angle for his next shot, so the
receiver's position is improved.

In making this shot it helps to think of playing the side of
the ball rather than, as usual, the back of the ball. On a
forehand, prepare out to the right, and literally hit the outside of the ball by swinging back to the left. On the backhand, prepare to the left, swing back to the right. If the
angle is a tough one and is getting away from you a little, do
not hesitate to use some wrist to get around outside it to
bring it back across the court. Preferably we'd like a smooth
stroke, but many times a good server, who can also put it
down the middle, surprises us a little and forces us to stretch
for the ball. The wrist is our last resort and, with a little luck,
can salvage many a tough situation.

This is one of many situations where technique is
modified by tactic. We think of a forehand as a back-and-
forth swing, but now it must be a right-to-left swing, almost
all of it being in front of us. There is no backswing: It is an
outswing followed by an inswing. It is almost impossible to
take the racket well back, come forward *and* get well around
the ball. The ball is way out to the side. We must play it
across the court almost as much as up and down the court.
Therefore, our swing must be a cross swing as contrasted
with a back-and-forth swing. Hold a ball on the forehand
side with your left hand. Try to come from directly behind
it and hit the right hand side of the ball. It is practically impossible. Now take your racket out and swing in on the ball.
It is easy to contact the right side. Your usual swing won't
do it. It must be modified. Now imagine a ball that is farther

out to the right so you are almost stretching for it. The only way to get around it is to use your wrist. Don't be afraid to do it and don't let anyone tell you, "That's wrong, you shouldn't use your wrist." Ideally the ball should never be allowed to get to that awkward spot—but it does, doesn't it? So use your wrist when in trouble. All the above applies equally to the backhand. It can be summed up by saying, "If you hope to swing in, you must first get your racket out." Or, "To play across the court, you must swing across the court."

RETURN AGAINST NET RUSHERS

A server who follows to net is saying, "I am going to force you, get in close, and put the ball away." The receiver's answer can take several forms. His first option is to stand back, take his time, and boom a big drive that he hopes will pass the server or be too tough for him. This is usually not a paying proposition. If the server is good at the net he will win because the receiver has allowed him to carry out his plan. He gets way in. If his serve is any good, consistent successful passing shots are impossible. This play will work only against erratic players or poor net players. It depends for success on the server's inadequacies rather than the receiver's good tactics. It is poor tactics on the whole—useful only to test out a player to see what he's got. It gives him a chance to miss, that's the best that can be said for it.

It may be suggested that the receiver can stand back, take his time, and play for the server's feet. This is equally ineffective since by giving the server time, the receiver allows the server to get in pretty close: There is little room between the server and the net, at least not enough to be an attainable target with any consistency. In other words, the receiver can't get it to his feet often enough to hope for success.

The only effective answer to a good plan is not to let it be carried out. The receiver must move in, take the ball early, and get it back as low as possible, but above all, as soon as possible, before the server can achieve a dominant position. If this can be done, the server has problems. He must volley a low ball from farther back. He has great difficulty in making a good enough first volley to ensure subsequent success. The receiver now has a good chance to come out on top in the exchange that follows.

Most players know all about this theory and agree that it is the best thing to do—but they can't do it with any consistency. Their usual explanation is, "I'm just not quick enough." This is seldom true. The real reason is that carrying out the tactic involves a modification of their customary technique. Not being aware of this, they try and try with their usual swing and fail and fail.

The most common quick return is a slice. It is usually referred to as a "chip." The word is very descriptive. The receiver moves in, takes the ball on the rise, and plays it with a short chopping stroke with the hope of dropping it at the server's feet. This has the dual effect of making him volley from far back, and also makes him volley a low ball.

The usual slice technique must be modified. The backswing must be almost completely eliminated: The racket is lifted out to the side but is *not* taken back. It is raised above and outside the ball and cuts down and in. The horizontal force is applied by the weight moving in: The receiver closes in and takes the ball as soon as he can without actually missing it. A second modification is that the face of the racket must be more closed. Why? Because a rising ball tries to ride high off the racket. It wants to pop up, and it must be held down. The usual sliced drive is made with a somewhat open face, off a ball that has reached or passed the top of its bounce. Scores of good players with steady slice backhands have trouble making an *early* return of service just because they take it with their rackets slanted the same as usual—and the ball goes too high and is a setup for a powerful first volley. They do not recognize that their usual method must be modified rather drastically or it won't work. They can return well by waiting longer—but this lets the server get way in so even a well-placed ball is a losing proposition.

It is important to make a mental contrast in picturing what is being done. For an ordinary backhand slice, a player takes his racket back and out, takes the ball at or after the top of the bounce, and cuts forward and across with a reasonably horizontal swing that goes down only a little as it comes across the ball. The face of his racket is somewhat open so the ball will rise and clear the net. For a chip return, a player lifts his racket decisively above the ball and chops down the back of the ball with an almost perpendicular racket face and swing. The problem now is to hold the ball down rather than to make sure it goes up. The two shots are quite different because a falling ball must be played up while a rising ball must be "covered" or it will pop up. The regular slice is back-out and forward-in—reasonably horizontal. The chip is up-out (no "back") and down-in, comparatively vertical (Figures 30, 31).

30

Backhand Chip Return

Figure 30: Note racket is high, outside, forward. Right foot is advanced and pointed sharply forward; racket face is comparatively closed (perpendicular). In Figure 31, note that racket has cut sharply down (this shot is a chop); simultaneously the

weight has pressed forward. The shoulders and left leg have
pivoted to take the ball cross-court (the percentage return).
This should be an early (note how far in he is) low, angled return—tough on the net rusher.

Many players like to try to sock a forehand return, but if they choose to chip, everything said above applies with equal force. One is primarily horizontal, the other primarily vertical, and the aspect of the racket face must be more closed for the chip.

Some readers may already have observed that what is being described is merely a chop. That is true, but there is great prejudice against the chop. "Don't chop the ball—*drive* it," is what we always hear. Yet even while the chop was being derided, many good players were "chipping" their service returns with considerable success, particularly on the backhand but also often on the forehand. In other words, the much-maligned and discarded chop, being a valuable and necessary shot, assumed another name and reappeared.

If a person cannot do anything else but chop, he is a limited player. But a chop or a chip—use whichever word pleases you—is a desirable shot to master and is of great value as a return of service. It is not the same as a slice drive and must be practiced as a separate technique. Its main relationship to the sliced drive is that both are cut shots. Otherwise it is very different.

THE DRIVE RETURN: THE BEST OF ALL

Now and then there appears a player with a backhand return that is not just good—it is devastating. Tony Trabert was known as "Terrible Tony" because he had this shot. If anyone was the greatest of all, it was Don Budge, who attacked every service, forehand or backhand, with hard topspin returns. Chris Evert (and years ago Alice Marble) constantly wrests the initiative away from the server with her powerful backhand returns. What have they got that the other fine players don't quite seem to have? Is it super-athletism, or is it a technique that can be learned? Can other good athletes hope to achieve such standout effectiveness? The answer is definitely that it is a matter of technique, not supertalent, and any good athlete can acquire the skill.

Many players can lash back a vicious topspin return with their forehands. Few can do it with their backhands. Why is this? Because the wrist can very naturally roll over the ball and keep a topspin return down even when taken on the rise. The wrist finds this very difficult to do on the backhand. Therefore, most players block flat or chip. They just can't topspin it and keep it down when it is rising. Their hand won't do it.

Here we come again to modification of technique. Both Trabert and Budge use a full eastern grip. The grip is not even a little continental (open-faced). This enables them to "cover" the ball and keep it down. They do not roll their wrist as they play. The racket is closed to start with and stays closed—the wrist doesn't have to turn the racket onto and over the ball. This is the trick: Get the grip (backhand) really fully on top of the racket so if it went any further, it would be a western. In preparing to play the ball, do *not* open the face—keep it closed a little, so the face plays above the center of the back of the ball. It is then possible—physically comfortable—to swing *up* from below a rising service and topspin it back without having it go too high. It is a completely natural backhand swing, from low to high, but the racket face is definitely more closed than on an ordinary drive played on a ball at or past the top of the bounce.

With a slight continental grip—used by many fine players —this is very difficult or impossible, even for a fine athlete. The wrist won't alter that much: You *must* change the racket.

There is a second modification of the usual drive technique that is forced on the receiver by the tempo. Good services get there pretty quickly. Also, the receiver is moving in and taking the ball early. There is no time for the full backswing one might ordinarily take. This is why so many say, "I'm not quick enough to do that." If they are attempting their usual moderately generous backswing they are right: They are not quick enough, and neither is anyone else. The backswing must be almost entirely eliminated. The racket is put to the side with the head a little down, and all the emphasis is put into the follow-through. Any backswing that occurs is caused by the turn of the shoulders as the player steps into the ball. It is almost (not quite) a block-and-follow-through shot. There is just enough approach to the ball to get the racket going, then it accelerates violently as it goes up the back of the ball in a high follow-through. The weight must be pressed forward or a fluffy, spinny, no-guts shot will occur. It is an aggressive shot, not a careful, get-it-back-shot (Figures 32–34).

The abbreviated backswing enables a receiver to prepare so quickly that he can be ready in time for anything less than a bullet serve. It is this abbreviation that makes him quick. He gets over the feeling that he is trying to do more than he has time for. Also, the near-zero backswing helps him to move in to get the ball early. It is difficult to move forward when you are swinging far back. The two moves— one forward, one back—tend to cancel each other out, so closing in is slowed. This is very important on higher-bounding serves. Once they get way up there, you can't play them well with any stroke—you can't get your weight onto them and you feel weak and ineffective. Whether you chip or topspin, never let a high bounder get really high, or you'll be in trouble.

All this sounds rather difficult and a little chancy. That is true. It is. But what are the percentages? You are up against a good player. He can volley and he has an overhead. He has practiced coming in behind his service for years. Do you think if you just put the ball back, that he will lose his serve? Will he miss *four* times, so you get the game? It is unlikely. The fact is you must *break* his serve by attacking it, by being a little reckless and playing for luck. You have everything to gain and nothing to lose, since he habitually wins his serve. If you can develop an aggressive topspin return on *both sides,* you are dangerous. Somewhere along the line you are going to get a hot streak wherein you whip the ball back at his feet and take the play away from him. This is what Budge and Trabert did. They didn't break service all the time—but they broke more than they got broken, and so were champions. A great first service, like Arthur Ashe's, will beat anyone when it's going in on a fast court. But no one, not even Ashe or Newcombe, gets that big first one in all the time. You get your chances. You should make something out of them, and you should develop the technique that will do it.

The greatest players have been, most often, those with the greatest return of service. They held service as well as others, but they broke more often. Laver and Connors are two recent examples of the truth of this statement. They don't have any better serves than many others, but watch their returns of service. That is where they are the best of

32

33

Backhand Topspin Return of Service

Important details: In Figure 32, the full eastern grip, slightly closed racket face, low preparation, no backswing (just a slight shoulder turn), semiopen stance, right foot advanced showing weight is moving forward, early interception of ball (note how far inside base line he is playing). Contrast this preparation with Figure 18 (Practice Backhand). Almost every aspect of the preparation has been modified to take the ball on the rise at higher

34

tempo. In Figures 33 and 34, the racket moves so violently upward that it takes the receiver up onto his toes in Figure 34
(some players will actually leap off the ground). Note that in
Figure 34 the left leg is just about to take a step, showing the
player has pressed forward with his weight while going up with
the racket. Altogether this is a violently aggressive return, calculated to wrest the initiative from the server.

the best and come out on top. Chris Evert does it too—and again is tops. She doesn't just get the ball back, she *booms* it back. The topspin return is the best of all.

The two-handed backhand lends itself to this play because it is essentially a left-handed forehand, and the left wrist can roll and cover the ball. Anyone with a one-handed backhand just about must use a full eastern grip or the ball will fly high. But either stroke must be used with a very reduced backswing and a closed racket face.

PERCENTAGES AGAIN

It has been stressed that to break up a well-conceived and well-executed plan necessitates taking chances. This is true, but there is no sense in going to extremes. It is hard enough to move in and take the ball on the rise—risking not even meeting it squarely—without adding to your problems. Therefore, the drive return should always be played back down the middle if the serve is to the middle, and cross-court right over the middle of the net the rest of the time. In other words, always take the biggest target. If you make an ace return, it should be luck: You aimed at the center and missed. Many good players try to win the point with their return, and they do, one out of three times. This won't win any games. It is also unconsciously very arrogant: I'm so good that even though you are a good server and a good volleyer, I am going to put the ball away the first time I hit it, each point. The fact is the server has the initiative, and this is an advantage. If you can establish parity with your first shot—as they say, "get into the point"—that is a major gain and should be the limit of your objectives beyond hoping for some occasional luck. If your ball is very low and provokes a weak half volley, you have even gained more, but don't count on it. To sum it up: Take the ball early, get it back quickly so he cannot get on top of you, and then scramble for the next one. Never mind having any delusions of grandeur about outright winners.

TAKING THE NET AWAY FROM THE SERVER

We stand roughly at the base line—which is behind the line with our toes close to it—to receive a strong service. Why do we stand there? Because if the server gets a deep service in near the back service line, we need that much time to judge the ball, prepare the racket, and step into the shot. But even good players don't *always* land the ball a foot from the line. If the ball lands short, the receiver can move in that much (whatever distance inside the back service line the ball lands) and still have the prescribed time to judge the ball and prepare. If it lands five feet or more short, the receiver can move in five or six feet inside the base line as he plays. This can well be a chance to attack.

Most players are not alert for such opportunities. If the ball lands short, they gratefully take more time to make their stroke, unaware that a chance to gain the initiative has been allowed to slip by. Actually, many servers, even good ones, are pretty careful with their second services. Many land short enough to be vulnerable. If such a service comes to the forehand, it should be walloped. If to the backhand, a chip or slice played for the feet of the in-rushing server can be followed right in. Volley it out with him. He is volleying up on his first shot—your chances are pretty good. If he is not coming to the net, you have options: Stay back and play deep, or attack down the line.

Here again mental attitude is of vast importance. If he makes a perfect service you're probably out of luck. Why worry about it? Isn't it better to think, "If he serves an imperfect one, I'm going to get him"? Search out chinks in his armor and exploit them, and above all make him feel you are after him, that you are a threat just waiting for a chance. Newcombe had Smith match point. Smith missed his first serve. Newcombe then stood so far to the left he had one foot in the alley. He as much as told Smith, "No matter what second serve you put in, I'm going to *smack* it with my forehand." Smith tried for the ace down the center, missed it, and Newcombe got the last point without playing a ball. Making your opponent feel a distinct threat whenever possible is excellent psychology as well as good tactics. It can work—even against Stan Smith.

RUNNING AROUND THE BALL

This is in line with the philosophy of being a little reckless and taking chances in order to break up the server's solid plan one way or another. If you have a powerful forehand, don't hesitate to run around a backhand and wallop the ball. In doing it, don't do it halfway. Just as the server is meeting the ball, take a *big* leap to the left (O.K., if he serves the other way, you are aced). This means you really get around it and can take a good swing and whale it aggressively. To do it less than completely usually means you don't get around it enough. The ball is too close, and you muff your shot or play weakly. Again, it is wise to play cross-court—for the big target—relying on your power to get your opponent in trouble. This play should be saved for important points. At 30–40, if the server misses his first ball, now is the time to take him by surprise, jump on him and get that game. There is no point in doing it when he has you 40–15: You merely show him your trick and doubtless lose the game anyway. Comparatively unorthodox plays such as rushing the net on his second serve, running around the ball, or on a clay court, when he is not rushing, to play a drop shot return—all these ploys that are a bit unusual depend on surprise, so they should be used only when the reward is great—winning a telling point.

VERSATILITY

Most players have one return of serve on their forehand and one on their backhand. Almost always such players will run into someone whose service "bugs" them. "I just can't seem to handle that particular serve." Or, "That serve gets me every time." This is almost inevitable when a player can handle the ball only one way, even if he does it quite well. The fact is, the server has the initiative and sets the pattern. The receiver must be adaptive and find an answer. If his one pet play isn't a good reply, he is out of luck.

Therefore, in returning service being able to go at the job in more than one way is more important than in any other area of play. Some topspin serves jump up so high it is very difficult to return a topspin: You can't seem to catch the ball low enough. But you can chip it down to his feet very nicely. Others come in with a lower bounce, and the topspin return works beautifully. A cannon ball can be best handled with a straight block, like a volley: Just put your racket flat on the ball, leaning into it, and it bang-boards right back, a nice crisp shot. Players who always try to swing can't handle a hard flat serve. They have no time for their swing. How much to crowd it, how much to swing, whether to chip or topspin or block—all these factors vary with different opponents.

Once a player has reached the "advanced" stage he should consciously set out to acquire the various tricks. The way to learn is to practice one at a time. Go out with someone who wants to practice his second serve, and play a hundred chips in succession, concentrating first on proper preparation (high, closed, no swing), then on moving in to chip it earlier and earlier. Another time do nothing but topspins, preparing low, closed, no swing. Swing right up very high and as you do so, lunge forward to get weight into it. Be sure your backhand grip is a full eastern. A lot, not a little, of drill on each is the only road to excellence because in actual play the tempo is fast. There is no time to think about how you do it—it must be practically a reflex, and this "muscle habit" state is only achieved through thousands of repetitions.

A good way to achieve the minimum backswing is to say to yourself "A little one" (swing) as the ball comes, then "And a big one" as you play it. Or, "A little one, move in, play." Talking to yourself is a good way to get your thought habits straight, and it is not possible to do the right thing unless you visualize it and think it correctly. If someone asks, "What are you mumbling about?" just say, "I'm brainwashing myself" and keep on growling as you practice. Above all, don't give up easily: Versatility is the greatest asset and the hardest to achieve.

PROGRESSION

If your return of service is limited to what one may call intermediate caliber and you wish to improve, go at it systematically. First emphasize stepping into the ball so you are getting your weight into it and it goes back a little more aggressively (without swinging any harder with your arm—it is just weight). Then try shortening your backswing and taking it even sooner. This involves new footwork. With the backhand, instead of putting your left foot to the side to get within reach, you move it diagonally forward, so that instead of stepping into it with one step you now have a step and a half. Emphasize this closing in effect until, on any serve that lands short, you jump in as far as you possibly can while still being able to judge and play the ball. Finally, try taking the net behind your return when the service is short.

As you push yourself to be ever more aggressive, you may find the ball will start to go back too high. You must cover it more by keeping the face of the racket perpendicular rather than open. You must do this as part of the preparation: It doesn't do, on the backhand, to try to get over the ball *after* you start to play it.

The racket must *be* closed before you play the ball. The key is to get ready properly; i.e., with a more closed racket face. Players tend always to think about how they mean actually to play the ball. They do not realize that it is not possible to play the ball correctly unless the racket is ready correctly. A player cannot prepare open and then play a closed shot. It seldom works. Therefore, getting one's mind concentrated on how one gets ready to play is a basic requirement in learning.

Eliminating most of the backswing is often very difficult. Think of it as a half volley. What do you do on a half volley? You trap the ball, with no swing, and you cover the ball by closing the racket face. You play the ball by lifting with a sharply upward follow-through, getting topspin on the ball as a result. Taking a service on the rise and topspinning it is about two thirds of the way from a regular drive toward a half volley, except that you play a half volley carefully—no speed because it is so low—and play the service much more aggressively because it is at or near net height. But the concept of the half volley, while of course too extreme, nevertheless gives a pretty clear idea of the necessary modification of technique needed to acquire an on-the-rise topspin return.

Sometimes learning by exaggeration helps. Stand a couple of feet behind the service line and return service from there. It certainly forces a player at once to be quick with his racket, to use a minimal swing, and to cover the ball with the racket.

Another good exaggeration is to have someone serve from the service line. (I believe this is a Chet Murphy drill. If so, he is to be complimented on the invention.) This is a good application of the overload principle: Make it twice as hard in practice. It is obvious that when someone is whacking serves from nineteen feet closer than normal, the receiver is forced to develop an extremely abbreviated technique and all the quickness that goes with it. Receiving a normal service then becomes easy by comparison.

Everything said about the backhand is equally true for the forehand. The best preparation is a closed racket face and very little backswing. However, some players with good wrists can prepare more open-faced, then whip over the ball with their wrist. It is possible to have less than perfect technique and often get away with it. But you'd better have a pretty good wrist, or it won't work. Correct racket preparation makes it possible for any player to make the shot. Only the most talented can go at it wrong and still often get it right; i.e., keep the ball down. That is why only the most talented can use a continental (open-faced) grip and still successfully topspin their return. Laver is a supreme example. But Laver has a tremendously strong and educated wrist. Do you?

THE OPEN MIND

Most people wish to and try to do things the best way. As a teacher the author has been asked a hundred times, "What do you think is the best way to return service?" This very question indicates a false premise: that there is such a thing as one best way. Actually there is no such thing. A tall man can take a ball higher with comfort than a short man. He therefore may take the ball at a different instant. A player endowed with very quick hands may crowd the service a bit more than the average person. Each player must adapt his techniques and tactics both to his opponents' play and his own talents. How, with my present skills, can I handle this fellow's service in such a way that he does not achieve an overwhelming advantage at each point? Since services vary from flat bullets to big high-bounding puff balls, it is impossible to give one answer for all situations.

There remains, however, the principle of the open mind. No player should ever say to himself, "This is the only way" —thereby closing his mind to other possibilities. He should say, "This is often the way, but not always. If it doesn't

work, I shall be alert to try anything else that offers hope."
It is perfectly all right to say, "I prefer this way"—whether
it's a chip, a topspin, or a flat block—just so long as the receiver does not close his mind to other ploys when in trouble.

Billy Talbert once sagely remarked, "For every punch
there is a counterpunch." Yes, *provided* you have acquired
the skill needed to execute the counterpunch. Since the
server has many options, it behooves the receiver to learn, as
nearly as he can, *all* the counterpunches, not just one. Basically there are the three techniques: the flat block, the chip,
and the drive. Advanced players should learn all three—then
they can adapt to whatever is thrown at them. Once this
versatility is achieved, the receiver can become a very
"smart" player, because if he has an idea, he can execute it.
He can play with imagination and variety, work on the
server almost as much as the server works on him, and frequently find a way to get a break. Versatility and an open
mind are basic to success in returning service in tournament
play, and the change to this attitude may be taken as one
distinction between an intermediate and an advanced
player.

V

Base-line Defense

This is a much neglected area in tennis thinking. Players and teachers tend to think that if a player has good base-line forehand and backhand strokes, he is automatically a strong defensive player. The player learning and the teacher teaching tend to work hard to reach that level of skill—and then stop. In advanced play this is an inadequate concept of defensive play. There is no reference to deception; going for the feet of the net player, the concealed lob, scrambling. Everyone recognizes these ploys as keys to successful defense, but few stress that, as in return of service, technical modifications of basic strokes are necessary if the execution is to be effective against a good net player. The skills need to be examined one by one.

TACTICS AND PERCENTAGES: PRESSURE

It is frequently noted that most points are lost, not won. Errors outnumber aces by a wide margin. Thus, one prime objective of the net player is to force his opponent into an error. He hopes to create a situation where the defender must give him a chance for an easy winner or try a shot that is too difficult for him. This is often referred to, psychologically, as, "Putting on the pressure." The attacker is saying, "You can't just hit the ball back, safely, way in, because

I'll put it away. You *must* try a tough shot. I'm betting you miss more than you make." This often is true. The defender is so afraid the attacker will make an ace if he can even touch the ball that he aims too fine and hits it out. Have we not all seen hundreds of passing shots—beautiful shots— that land a foot into the alley because of this fear? The first thing to learn—and often the hardest—is to keep the ball in the court, to give one's self a large enough target so that errors are not numerous. Many players who are very steady when their opponent stays back are prone to error when he puts the pressure on them by going to net.

But, he counters, the pressure is real. He *will* put the ball away if I just hit it back. What else can I do except aim for the lines? He can do a lot, and that is what he must learn and substitute for his one-in-and-two-out tactics. He can be deceptive, hiding his shot so that a decent shot can be a winner (as contrasted with a line splitter). He can keep the ball low, hoping to give the attacker a tough volley very difficult to turn into a winner. He can thus hope to transfer the pressure: Now the attacker may try a shot that is too tough for him and make an error. He can incorporate the lob into his defense, thus making the attacker more hesitant about closing in for the kill: He must guard the back door. As will be brought out, these skills are closely interrelated. Clearly, if he fears the lob, he will linger a bit farther back. Now the passing shot gets past him or dips to his feet and gets him into trouble. If he worries about the cross-court and closes in to cut it off, the lob may float over his head. If the ball is kept low, he may have great difficulty in acing the defender even if he is there for the shot. The defender has a chance to scramble and get another try. Thus, a well-equipped defender can turn it into a battle of wits and have a good chance of coming out on top. The pressure is now divided: The attacker feels equally that he too *must* make very fine shots or this fellow will beat him. So he too may make some errors. Things even up a bit.

This all reads like fun. Bring on your attackers—we'll take them apart, tie them in knots, make them flub, fake them out of their sneakers. Fortunately, it is not that easy. The attacker has the initiative and often forces the defender so vigorously that he cannot do much except lob. The defender's options are restricted by the physical pressure of the attacking shot. But on every occasion when a good return of service provokes an ordinary rather than a near-winning first volley, and on every occasion when the attacker's approach shot leaves something to be desired, the defender does have an opportunity to break up and overcome the attacker. Seizing these chances and making much of them means one player achieves more service breaks than the other.

DECEPTION: QUICK PREPARATION

One of the most deceptive measures is to wait, or hesitate a little, just before playing a passing shot or a lob. If the defender hesitates, the attacker must wait also. He tends to stop and become doubtful as to which way he is going to have to move—he may even make a wrong move. Either way his anticipation is impaired or misled. All players have experienced this, to their chagrin when on the receiving end. It sounds like an easy trick to acquire, but it isn't because of tempo. The defender must be there, racket and feet prepared, *before* the ball arrives, otherwise he cannot wait and upset his opponent's rhythm of movement and thought. When the play is at all high caliber there doesn't seem to be any extra time. The defender must create this time by being even quicker than he apparently has to be to make his shot. One must work on it to be that quick.

A good analogy is a snake. At the first suspicion of danger or prey, he *instantly* coils up prepared to strike. He usually doesn't strike immediately unless he must in self-defense, but he is ready, and it is then difficult to tell just when he actually will commit himself. And when he does it is sudden, quick, leaving no time for a dodge or a countermove by his victim. Many people don't like snakes, but they are very efficient at quick preparation and the sudden strike. Wouldn't you like to have poisonous passing shots? Then imitate the snake. He's the best, because he is always ahead of the ball.

This goes right back to what we taught beginners: racket ready, wait, play. But it is now at a higher tempo, with feet and racket reacting the instant the ball leaves the opponent's racket. It may be remarked in passing that preference was given this method just because it lends itself to deception in defense and offense. This is also why teachers are forever saying, "Get your racket ready sooner—sooner." They are anticipating that later you may be playing at a faster tempo, when a slow and deliberate preparation is useless because there isn't time for it: The ball gets there too quickly. Now even more quickness is demanded, so even though the ball comes fast—and attackers are seldom gentle in their attack—some of that very little time is left over, after the preparation, for that deceptive *wait*.

Another large benefit to be derived from quick preparation is that it increases the defender's options. If he barely reaches the ball, he can often play it well in only one way. His opponent senses this, anticipates, and volleys a winner. If the defender is ahead of the ball, he can choose any of his four options: low for the feet, straight, cross-court, or lob. Conversely, it may almost be said that without this quickness in setting up no effective defense is possible over a large number of points. A defender must be determined that no matter how fast the ball comes, he will be faster.

DECEPTION: IDENTICAL PREPARATION

Every attacker studies his opponent, watching for mannerisms that enable him to "read" what he plans to do. If there is any giveaway, he is sure to spot it, and the defender wonders how this fellow can always be there to volley his passing shot or smash his lob.

Many players think that they should "fake." That is, they make what they hope are misleading motions calculated to lead the attacker up the garden path and leave him there, hopelessly out of position. This is a poor method. It will often work once or twice, but that's all. The attacker soon figures out, "When he makes that move what he really means is the other," and he is there for it. Also, unnecessary moves often impair execution, and the defender fakes himself into an error. Faking is not the best solution.

The real answer is identical preparation. If a defender sets up exactly the same way whether he intends to play straight, cross-court, or lob, the attacker has no clue as to which will actually happen. The feet, shoulders, and racket should be the same, every time. And they must be totally the same, not just nearly the same. If a defender turns away even a little extra to play straight rather than cross-court, the attacker will soon be reading him successfully. The perfect crime leaves *no* clue.

How can one set up always the same? By always preparing to play straight. When we swing, the body always turns from the outside in. That is, from right to left for forehands and from left to right for backhands. It is very easy to set up for a straight shot, then pivot while playing (not before) and make a cross-court. The pivot, if withheld until the last minute, occurs too late to be "read" with much profit. From the same setup one can lob if one wishes.

Identical preparation has an added virtue. Besides making the attacker guess or move late, it enables the defender to groove his technique in the most simple way, and we all know simplicity and consistency go together. The defender does *nothing* unusual or extra difficult. He gets ready to play straight—and pivots cross-court just as he plays. Or, he gets ready to play straight—and at the last instant picks the ball up with a hidden lob. He decides what he is going to do, and simply goes ahead and does it. His opponent may guess, but he has no way of *knowing*. This is the easiest for the defender and the toughest for the attacker—and that's the objective. The best base-line defenders do this, and seem to fool you with maddening simplicity. Hasn't it happened to you? Well, learn to dish it out as well as to take it. It is much more fun to do it than to be victimized by it.

A ball machine is great for drilling this skill. Set the machine to play a fair shot to the side—one that creates a little pressure but not much. Stand at the center of the base line and just practice moving and setting up for the straight shot every time, but vary what you actually do. The point of the drill is to concentrate on your preparation, so it is always the same. After that is achieved, then experiment with how much you must pivot and come around the ball to get a good angle cross-court, how long you can delay the pivot and still actually get it cross-court, how long you can delay dropping the racket below the ball to lob. After a while it should be possible for you to set up very quickly *and* always the same way. Thus, quick preparation is combined with a totally concealed intent, and you are on your way to developing a good defense.

THE SHORT STROKE AND EXTRA SPIN

Ordinary base-line drives, when both players are back, should be smooth, deep, and solid. The ball travels quite high over the net, and stays up until it passes the service line, then dips to land near the base line. This is the best possible shot both offensively and defensively. But such a shot is a poor passing shot unless it is a clean winner: The attacker doesn't even get his racket on it. It is definitely overly optimistic to hope for a large percentage of such total success. It is much more realistic to give the attacker his due and figure he will get to many or most of your attempted passes. If the regular base-line shot is used, he will have a rather high-level ball to play, above the net, so he can play hard directly down at the court without hitting the net. If he is a good aggressive volleyer, the defender is out of luck. As the saying goes, he will get killed. The better play is to shorten one's stroke, take a lot of length off the ball, use more than normal topspin, play closer to the top of the net, and try to make the ball dip as soon as it crosses the net, so if it were not volleyed it would land inside the service line.

In other words, play as low and as short as risk will permit. This is a good general rule with one exception: When forced very wide, the deep pass enables one to keep the ball farther away from the net players on the straight shot.

This is quite different from a deep base-line shot. The swing is shorter and more sudden, the racket face is slightly more closed to cover the ball and keep it down, and the follow-through is less lengthy and full—it is more nearly a quick-up-yank that gives more spin and less carry or length (Figures 35, 36). This type of shot can still be a clean winner if the attacker moves the wrong way. But even if he doesn't, it is a tough ball to put away. A sharply dipping ball is notoriously more difficult to volley than a level ball. A ball below the net cannot be volleyed hard and kept in the court. The attacker is inhibited in his desire to kill. He can put it away, yes, but only by means of an extremely skillful placement. The defender always hopes he has a winner, but even if he fails to fool the attacker, he is still in the point. The necessarily slower volley gives him a chance to scramble, make another try, or sneak a lob over the attacker's head. Playing this way he can aim a little farther in, reducing his own errors, playing more to get the other fellow in trouble rather than to put upon himself the pressure of attempting a clean pass.

It should be noticed that this altered stroke technique strongly reinforces what has already been advised; namely, a quick preparation and a hesitation or wait just before launching the shot. The shorter backswing can be accomplished quicker than a long one. The shorter actual hit can be held until the last instant. Thus, beside the insurance policy of the lower-dipping ball, this technique enhances deception.

BALANCE AND FOOTWORK

It is a characteristic of strong defenders that they have quiet rackets and very active feet. The more they have to run for a ball, the more they will curtail their swing. Anyone can make a comparative trial. Pretend you are dashing for a wide ball, and as you dig try taking a big swing. The loss of poise and balance is at once apparent, and you are markedly slowed down. The reason is obvious: The swing of the arm and racket taking a full backswing is a force that conflicts with, impedes, and reduces your progress toward the ball. The conflict not only reduces the overall result, but makes you feel awkward and clumsy as well. It is as though some- one had hold of your shirt tail and was holding you back. You are fighting yourself. For contrast, start from the same place, and as you take your first step, reach out toward the ball with the arm and racket. All forces are now pulling and pushing toward the same spot—where you will intercept the ball. Poise, balance, and smooth moving are maintained, awkwardness tends to disappear. You arrive sooner, the racket head is nearer the ball, you are poised and can there- fore aim well, and a quick sharp deceptive shot is possible. Actually, the principle is very simple: The more a player tries to do the more time he needs to do it. In pressure cases such as described above, a player doesn't have time to do any more than the absolute minimum necessary to play the ball. Reducing one's technique to this irreducible minimum is the key to playing under pressure.

35

Base-line Passing Shot

In the preparation (Figure 35), note the rather short backswing, the slightly closed racket face, the wide-open stance that will make possible a quick recovery. In Figure 36, note the high follow-through, indicating heavy topspin was applied to the ball:

He is already moving back to his left to recover position. Contrast this illustration with the forehand normally taught to beginners (Figure 15). Also note how closely akin this skill is to that of Figure 26 (Topspin: Basic Drive).

SMALL STEPS

Beside the almost motionless racket extended toward the ball, there is another essential to success in making a running passing shot. This is to take quick small steps rather than huge lunging strides. A player's feet must be under him when he arrives if he is to have the poise needed for an accurate shot. He must get there, yes, but he must arrive *on balance*. If he arrives with one foot way out in front and the other straddled back somewhere behind—his feet wide apart —his ability to make an exact passing shot or lob will be seriously impaired. He will look, feel, and actually be comparatively awkward. If for those few huge stretching steps he substitutes more numerous quicker but smaller steps, he will not only get there faster (stretching merely strains you, it doesn't move you), but will feel under control—i.e., on balance—when he plays the ball. Perhaps the neatest mover in the game is Rosewall. He is small, does not have unusual power, does not have a great service—in fact, what does he have? He has perfect balance at all times, so that even when sorely pressed he *always* is able to play the ball at the top of his form. He takes quick, small steps, never overswings, and can stand almost any amount of pressure. Until age caught up with him, he was practically an iron curtain that few could ever break down. He is a man whose style of moving is worthy of imitation by one and all. We hear much of his backhand. We should hear more of his perfect balance, which means that on every shot he is neatly ready to do his best. This is true also of his volleying, which is as near impeccable as can be. His perfect poise at all times, even when running full out, is the foundation for his amazing consistency, offensively and defensively, match after match, through a long career. He takes quick small steps.

Many years ago Sarah Palfrey (now Mrs. Danzig) won two national championships. Everyone commented on how neat and poised she always looked—a true delight to watch on the court. Her popular nickname? "Twinkle Toes." There it is again—quick small steps. An admirer of the legendary Big Bill Tilden once remarked, "His footwork is funny. He seems to take a lot of mincing little steps. Why does he do that?" Put that comment together with the fact that Tilden had probably the greatest running, passing shots in the history of the game. He made show-stopping aces against great net players off both wings on the dead run when one wondered if he would even reach the ball. He reached the ball, *and* he was perfectly balanced as he arrived, so he made as fine a shot as he would have if someone had played the ball within easy reach.

A quiet racket, held to the side (*not* back) as one runs, plus quick small steps and a low crouch—all these can be practiced just like anything else. A ball machine is excellent for this purpose: Set it to play toward a corner, start far enough from it so there is some difficulty in reaching the ball, then do it. Concentrate on one thing at a time: first, the motionless racket extended toward the ball, with just barely enough last-instant backswing to get the racket going enough to play the ball; second, talk to yourself, saying, "Step, step, step" as fast as you can, and see if you can make your legs do it that fast; third, do all in a deep crouch, so if you reach the ball at the last second before it bounces twice you are down there with it and can also get good leg drive and lift into the shot. If you really do it seriously, it is a tough drill—you should get tired. If it isn't tough, you are starting from too close: move back, make it tougher. Practice your three options: straight, cross-court, lob. The ideal toward which you are striving is, "If I can reach the ball at all, I should be able to play it well." Very few players can do this.

SCRAMBLING: THE TWO-SHOT PLAY

Isn't this subject just what we have finished discussing? In part, yes, but there is another aspect of it that has not been touched on. This is scrambling for the next shot. Tactically, it has been pointed out, it is the height of conceit to plan on a clean passing shot that ends the point, leaving you victorious without further effort. Good net players are hard to fool. They hold their position. They cover everything except real needle threaders. It is therefore highly probable that the attacker will indeed reach the ball and play it. That is why so much stress has been placed on making it a dipping shot that is hard to put away. The realistic fact is that the defender may hope he gets a winner, but he should *plan* on being prepared to play again. The clean winner, when it occurs, should be a pleasant surprise. It should never be counted on. A good return of service against a net rusher or a first try at a pass should be considered successful if it thwarts the attacker's hope for a winner and causes him enough trouble to oblige him to give the defender a decent second chance with perhaps a little more time to set up and play with more deadly accuracy.

THE OPEN STANCE ON THE FOREHAND

There is often controversy about this. Many maintain that the square or closed stance is the correct way to play the ball, and that the open stance is wrong. This is true for beginners and intermediates who are learning the basic mechanics of the game and have not yet related to tactical situations and shot sequences. Advanced players are constantly relating to tactics and, as has been repeatedly pointed out, must frequently modify technique to serve a tactical purpose.

The open stance on the forehand offers several advantages. There is economy of effort: Putting the right leg out gets the hitting arm within reach of the ball. Putting the left foot forward is extra effort, and a player must move the left leg back again to start his recovery. Thus, there is economy of time. Using a closed stance makes for a much slower recovery. This is crucial and decisive in good play because the tempo is so fast. That is why a majority of class players use the open stance when defending against a net rusher (Figures 35–38).

Why teach beginners the closed stance? Because we want them to get their shoulders sideways so they will turn into the shot and apply their weight. The closed stance is the easy comfortable way to do it. Is it possible to get shoulder turn and weight into the ball using an open stance? Yes, it is. It is done by twisting at the waist. This allows one to have one's cake and eat it too. The advantages of the closed stance are obtained, *and* the first step (left foot) of the instant recovery has already been taken—a very great advantage when microseconds differentiate between success and failure. Thus, the open stance improves a player's chances to achieve the ideals already discussed—instant preparation, wait before hitting, short backswing—and it also speeds the scramble for the next shot.

Why is the open stance almost never used on the backhand? Because what must be done is to get the playing arm within reach of the ball. We use the same arm for both forehand and backhand. It is hung on our right side, over the right leg. So for a forehand we put the right leg to the right to reach the ball, and on the backhand we put the right leg to the left to reach the ball—using here a closed stance in most cases.

THE SLIDER

Again some modification of racket skill is sometimes desirable. It is possible to take the ball a little early, as though playing cross-court, and yet play down the line by using a laid-back wrist, which allows the ball to slide to the right on the forehand and to the left on the backhand. (Figures 37, 38). The popular name for the shot is very descriptive—the ball does seem to slide off for a straight shot although the swing says cross-court. This not only aids deception, but again speeds recovery because the defender is facing more toward the net and less toward the side as he plays: He gets a faster start back the other way. The deception is excellent: identical setup, identical contact point, with the only readable sign being that the racket comes around the ball at the instant of playing it for a cross-court—or the wrist doesn't come around and the ball goes straight.

It is obvious beginners can't be taught such advanced techniques. But advanced players can and should learn these tricks. Watch the top players. They do this sort of thing constantly: Slide it down the line or hook it cross-court, both executed at the last instant so the net player can't tell and has to guess. All top players hide their shots.

At this point it is worthwhile to point out the versatile use of the wrist involved in these skills. There is a great tendency among teaching pros to blare forth the pronunciamento, "Never use your wrist in stroking a tennis ball!" This is good advice for beginners, who tend to flap at the ball loosely and meaninglessly and fail to achieve a co-ordinated swing of the body, arm, and racket. But we should not forget the adage, "Rules are made to be broken"—*after* you know them. An advanced player, in sharp contrast to a beginner or intermediate, should not hesitate to use all his assets, and one of his assets is his wrist. Is it accidental that the great Rod Laver, the winningest of the winners, is noted for using a "lot of wrist"? Is it accidental that there never has been a prominent player who didn't have a good wrist? Let us train our beginners soundly, but let us not put them permanently in irons after they become advanced. The wrist is a major asset and should be used whenever it will enhance our skills.

To drill scramble it is hard to beat the two-on-one exercise, where one baseliner plays two net players who yank him from side to side as fast as he can go. The baseliner learns to play-and-take-off for the other side, rather than play and linger sluggishly. Co-ordinating the instant recovery and reversal of direction with good execution takes a lot of work.

37

Backhand Slider

This looks like a cross-court. It is meant to, and it could be. But if the wrist is kept laid back so the racket plays the inside of the ball, the shot can be directed down the line. Known as a "slider," this shot can be alternated with one in which the wrist is brought around the ball to carry it cross-court. The ad-

vantage of this combination is that it permits the use of the open stance, which gives a quicker recovery of position: The feet, body, and racket move to the right; only the ball goes left. Many fine players use sliders. Very few pros ever teach them.

THE LOB

Integrating the lob into defensive base-line play is of extreme importance. It is a total fallacy to say, "No point in lobbing—he has a great overhead." The fact is that the lob is what makes possible successful passing shots. If an attacker does not have to worry about the lob, he is free to close far in where he can easily put away every ball he can reach. There is no room between him and the net that the defender can exploit with a dipping passing shot. The attacker never volleys into the net due to being caught a little too far back. Everything goes his way—he has a big day, and the defender finds himself frustrated at almost every turn.

It helps in defense to have a plan. If the first try—whether return of service or a try at a passing shot—fails to get the attacker in trouble and he makes a good first volley, it is a good rule to lob the second shot. Why? Because the attacker on the first shot has probably not reached his full forward position, and is far enough back so a lob cannot get over him. But, after his first volley he is all the way in, hoping for the kill, so now there is some room behind him. Thus, even if the first volley does not press him much, the defender should often lob. This means lob by *choice*, not because you can't do anything else.

The big booming shots are what everybody notices and applauds. Few people realize that some of the greatest attackers were masters of the lob. Big Jake ("High Pockets") Kramer and Pancho Gonzalez, probably the two greatest exponents of the invincible serve and the infallible deadly overhead—both these "all attack" players were ever conscious of the importance of the lob and used it constantly. Once when they met in a match, Kramer was asked, after winning in five sets, what his game plan had been. Kramer replied that he had decided to lob Gonzalez constantly, hoping hitting so many overheads would take a lot out of him as the match wore on. There is a world champion's strategy against a player with a truly great overhead. Doubtless this is an unusual case. But it is to be noted that two perennial winners, Rosewall and Laver, both could and did constantly lob with beautiful concealed touch. If anyone crowded the net to cut off their passing shots, they at once resorted to that tantalizing floater—a deep lob. This constant threat kept their opponents a step or so back, and the passing shots became effective again.

The young player tends to forget about the lob. It just isn't part of his thinking. And if his opponent kills one convincingly, he mutters, "That's enough of that fool shot" and lobs no more. What he does not realize is that the lob, even if killed, is still necessary if his passing shots are to be successful. The short backswing preparation makes possible great concealment. Just as the forward swing is begun the head of the racket is dropped and comes from below the ball to lift it high. It is a very good idea in drilling defense, as previously outlined, to lob at least every third shot. This not only perfects the technique but also helps it become a thought habit so it is there, in the mind, during a hard match.

Often a sacrifice play can be effective. If a server is closing in and killing the ball, plan to lob almost every shot for a whole game. Even if he kills them all, he will start lingering back for them. The next time he serves, a reversion to more aggressive play may bring a break—he isn't on top of the net anymore. Whether this extreme use of the lob is preferred or not, it is important to appreciate and never forget that the lob is the only play that prevents him from closing far in where his advantage is too great to be overcome any other way. An impetuous player who rushes way in all the time can be destroyed by good lobbing. And even a more judiciously aggressive player can be forced to mind the back door enough to leave a crack open up front.

THE IMPORTANCE OF DEFENSE

As a general statement (i.e., one admittedly subject to exception), it is true that defense tends to be neglected. The attack somehow is more appealing to youth. Defense means pooping or being afraid to hit the ball. "The best defense is a good offense" is a very popular way of disposing of the whole problem. Or, "If I win my serve, how can I lose?" The young man or woman with talent is much more preoccupied with service, volley overhead, and other weapons of attack than with the art of defense.

It is better to deal with facts. It is a fact that by the rules the other fellow serves half the time. Any player is in the defensive position half the time by law, whether he prefers it or not. It is also a fact that if a player's game is all offense, he can hope only for a tie breaker—a very chancy thing. And who wins tie breakers? The player who can get an extra point or two on the other fellow's serve.

A very brief review of the greats of the past reveals an eye-opening coincidence. Almost all the greatest players—the champions of champions—had phenomenal defensive skill. Tilden, LaCoste, Perry, Budge, Kramer, Gonzalez—all had superb defensive skill and won over the other winners of their time because of it. It is not the province of this book to go into a long dissertation on the styles of historical greats, so it is appropriate to leave that statement and jump to the present. Have not Laver and Rosewall been the most consistent winners? Does either of them have one of the greatest serves? No. Their serves are only adequate. It is their defense that is outstanding. They break serve—defend successfully—more often than any of their rivals, and have done so over almost a couple of decades. And today who dominates women's tennis? Is Chris Evert the greatest attacker? Does she have the greatest serve and net game? Quite obviously it is her base-line skill—defensively as well as offensively—that puts her above her rivals, some of whom are better than she is at net. What is the most phenomenal thing about Jimmy Connors' phenomenal game? His return of service—a hard topspin ball right to the net player's feet every time. No one has done it better since Don Budge in his prime forty years ago, slew all comers with his lethal returns.

It can almost be said that the greatest players are those that are the greatest serve breakers. Obviously this is an exaggeration, but there is great truth in it. And it is not an overstatement to proclaim that defense in tennis, as in football, is at least half the game. Advanced players who hope to become successful tournament players—that is, *very* advanced players—would do well to put at least half their time on developing defensive skills. The greatest players have seldom been unbalanced. They had *both* a strong offense and a a strong, skillful defense. Quite often their attack was less impressive than that of some of their rivals, as in the case of Rosewall, but their defense was just about always very tough. Rosewall's return of service and his backhand passing shot were the talk of the circuit when he was at his peak.

It would be a fine thing for the game if there were more written about defensive tricks and the techniques needed to execute them. There has always been a great outpouring about service, volley, and basic ground strokes. Recently the neglected half-court area has received considerable attention. But all the skills, tricks, deceptions, and variations of superb defensive play seem by comparison to receive little if any emphasis. Isn't this a marked error of omission? Surely there is much more to be said than I have put down here. Many others have ideas of their own, so what has been said here should be taken as a starter, not an attempt at the last word.

VI

Half-court Shots

THE COMMON FALLACY

An improving player who becomes reasonably proficient at the base-line rally soon finds himself winning the rally quite frequently. The other fellow makes a poor return; that is, a short ball that invites attack. It is a fact that the majority of competent young players are unable to take advanage of such a slip by their opponent. It can be said that the distinction between a good player and a "promising" player is that the good player can hurt you when you make a mediocre base-line return; the promising player cannot. One can even go so far as to say that the easiest way to beat many steady baseliners is to pull them in—i.e., make a short shot on purpose.

This seems most peculiar. How can it be that a bad shot can be more effective than a good deep shot? This is true because most players seldom if ever practice handling short shots. They assume that the forehand and the backhand they have learned at the base line will handle adequately all forehand and backhand situations. This is a fallacy. It ignores the fact that this is a different situation requiring rather sharp modifications of the usual base-line techniques.

A base-line shot is played comparatively high over the net. A half-court or approach shot must be played lower over the net or it will go out because it has less distance to go: A good part of the court is now behind the striker, not still in front of him. This difference is often ten to twenty feet. Therefore, a player must prepare his racket a little higher behind the ball, and the face of his racket must be more closed. He prepares to play as level as he can without striking the net, instead of up well away from the net. For the same reason—restricted length—a player's swing should be shorter in the half-court area. A long swing produces a long shot, but here we do not want such a long shot since it will go out. Thus, the racket should be prepared closer to the ball: less backswing.

In a base-line rally—both players back—there is little opportunity for deception. It is a sparring contest rather than an attack-against-defense situation. By contrast, it is important to hide one's shot when attacking a short ball. If an opponent can read the attacker's plan, he can get a good start and put into effect all the base-line defensive skills discussed in the previous chapter. If he is kept in doubt until the ball is actually played, he is denied this extra time, and his defensive capabilities are hampered. Hopefully he is pressed and rushed enough so that the attack is successful in forcing him to return a ball that can be volleyed or smashed for a winner or a near winner. This is often referred to as "getting him off balance," but what is this if not another way of saying, "keeping him in doubt until the last instant"? Just as in defensive play a short quick backswing, a wait, a suddenly released shot, plus identical preparation no matter what shot is intended are the secrets to a deceptive attack. The skills needed for deception do not change just because we are attacking rather than defending (Figure 39).

The Approach Shot and Deception

Note that the racket is high and closed, so the shot will be much more of a net skimmer than a normal deep drive. Also, the backswing is short, and the stance is two-thirds open. From this preparation the player can play a slider down the line, a crosscourt, or a drop shot, and can (due to open stance) get a fast start in behind his shot if he wishes to follow it—all with no giveaway.

The open stance on the forehand, or rather a semiopen diagonal stance, is very useful when attacking. A player can lean into his approach shot and be instantly running in behind it. A fully closed stance slows the follow-up. When attacking a short ball a player does not merely play the ball. He plays the ball *and* gets to net. Getting to net must be part of the shot, not something that happens later. Co-ordinating the forward move with the follow-through of the shot is an important technique peculiar to approach shots, just as recovery of position is an important technique in defensive base-line play. The player must learn to hit, step, step, step—not just to finish hitting, then set about moving in. A player who has mastered this skill gives the impression that he plays the ball and *is* at net. If his shot hits the net for an error, he is up there to pick up the ball while muttering to himself to aim a bit higher.

Thus, attacking shots from the half-court area have their own technique and must be practiced separately if excellence is to be achieved. The instant preparation, the wait, and the sudden deceptive release are the same as for baseline defensive shots, but there are new aspects: the higher more closed racket and the co-ordinated forward move to net position that becomes part of the shot.

In drilling these forcing shots it is very important to be realistic. The player should play-and-advance, so when he finishes he has crossed the service line. It is unwise to practice the shot and the move separately, because the forward move, being a part of the shot, tends to carry the ball deeper. A player who practices the shot without following it, and then uses it in play, will find himself frequently playing over the base line when he follows it during a real point.

Only by practicing the two together does he learn to allow for this so as to keep his hard shot in bounds.

An excellent drill, and one that is fun, is to play with new rules: Whoever is serving must serve underhand and give the receiver a setup. The receiver must attack and follow to net. The server may then use (and practice) all his defensive skills while the attacker tries to finish him off. It is real tennis in reverse. The server should never win. It is extraordinary how often he does win because his opponent has not perfected his ability to capitalize fully on a mistake. The value of this upside-down tennis is that it eliminates both the serve and the base-line rally—everyone gets lots of that anyway—and forces on both players the skills they tend to neglect: approach shots and base-line defense. To win one's service is to achieve a "break." The match can be hotly contested and lots of fun, and it certainly tends to round out technique and tactics besides providing variety. It is recommended particularly to all who play a lot on slower courts such as clay or fast-dry.

The drill can be refined and made more specific by changing the rules. The server must set up the ball every time to the receiver's backhand, or to his forehand, or in the center. Thus, if a player has a good attack with his forehand but is not skillful with his backhand, the drill can be focused on the weakness. Every point (when he receives) must start with the shot he hopes to perfect: backhand slice approach, for example. Of course, it must be a rule that he may not run around it.

This drill is particularly valuable to two types of players: one who is very steady but reluctant to move in, and one who has a "big game" but little defensive proficiency. Both

Backhand Slice Approach

A repeat of Figures 27–29 (Slicing a Backhand) is purposely used here because no changes are needed in this technique, except that for a very low ball, the entire sequence would be executed in a deeper crouch. The big point that cannot be overstressed is that the racket moves from left to right, the weight from back to front. There is *zero* backswing: The racket is prepared out, then cuts in. There is thus an outreach and an inpull, not a backswing and a forward swing. The forward motion of the racket occurs because the weight moves and carries everything with it. Note that the player is on his way with the ball.

can profit enormously from playing in this apparently bizarre manner that eliminates the service and the rally and forces them, every point, to do that which they are least capable of doing. The steady but timid player builds confidence in his attack, and the big hitter develops defensive skill and pride.

TACTICS

An attacker has two choices: He can play what is theoretically the most sound shot, or he can attack a weakness every time even if so doing violates theory. The soundest shot, when the short ball is to one side or the other of the court, is to play straight and go straight in behind it. If the ball is in the center, one has three choices. Obviously, the attacker can play to either side. But he can also play straight down the middle. This, the "center theory," is much touted because it reduces the defender's possible angles. But two facts militate against it. One, it leaves the defender in perfect position: No opening is created that can be exploited by the subsequent volley. Two, it assumes that the defender is so strong on both sides that the attacker is afraid to test either of them. Bill Tilden was that good off both wings, and many preferred to attack him down the center. How many others? Is your opponent that totally fearsome, and are you such a great volleyer you can beat him even if he is in perfect position? It is generally a better plan to place the approach shot to one side, thus opening the other side. The attacker can then volley for the opening or behind the defender as he rushes to cover the opening.

Why should the attacker play straight rather than crosscourt? Because he can then go straight forward behind his shot and attain the maximum forward position before he must check his rush so as to be ready to break left, right, or back for a lob when the defender plays. If he plays crosscourt, his alley is wide open. He cannot go forward except very diagonally. He does not get as far in. Moreover, if the defender plays cross-court, the attacker is often caught going the wrong way as he moves to cover the open alley. Also, the cross-court-approach shot takes longer to get past an opponent. The straight shot gives him less time—it is "on him" quicker. The pressure is greater. Therefore, the cross-court is advisable only when an opponent is much stronger off one side than the other, so the gain outweighs the theoretical loss.

It should not be concluded from this that every forehand approach shot goes to the backhand of the opponent. Many short balls are so near the center that the attacker has a clear choice. In such a situation it is profitable often to attack the defender's forehand just because he tends to expect the attack to go to his backhand. It is also desirable on a few occasions to make the "wrong" shot (i.e., cross-court) just to keep the defender in doubt and hamper his anticipation.

Some setups are very near the side line or even a trifle into the alley. In such cases it is difficult to make an effective straight shot because one must play somewhat back toward the defender in order to hit the court. But due to the location of the ball, it is possible to make an extremely sharp angle cross-court—almost to the corner of the service court— a shot that pulls the defender far out of position or even is a winner if surprise is achieved. This is often a good choice. Whether it should be followed to net is a matter of judgment. If the attacker thinks he can cover the open alley, and if he has his opponent in enough trouble to force a weak return, then he should follow the shot in. If not, he may choose to retreat to the base line, counting on running him again with the next shot.

THE SLICED APPROACH

The easiest half-court shots are those off a ball that bounces to or above net height. Such a ball to the forehand can be hit very hard and kept in bounds consistently. On the backhand very few players can hit a hard backhand topspin approach shot. Most prefer to slice. Moreover, many short balls do not bounce high. They are shots that go lower than intended, skim over the net, land short, and bounce low. The slice is just about the *only* effective way to play these on either the forehand or backhand.

The cleaner topspin shot depends on speed for its effect. It is a "rock 'em and sock 'em" play. But if a low ball is hit that hard, it will either go out or in the net. The angle of elevation to clear the net is too sharp to enable one to give the ball real power and still come down inside the base line. The slice is not a speedy shot. It is effective because of its mean, low, kicking bounce. The kick bothers the defender's timing and touch, and above all, the low bounce forces him to hit up. It is a fact that it is at least twice as difficult to make a good passing shot from a low ball as off a higher bounce. A further advantage is that the slower flight of the slice enables the attacker to reach better net position: He has more time. Thus, it is no wonder that most accomplished players slice all approaches except high bouncers to their forehand, and some even slice or chip those.

The technique on this shot must emphasize the fact that slicing a low ball is a crossing motion, from the outside in, not a back-and-forth motion. The racket is prepared out to the side and pulled in sharply across the back of the ball.

This spins the ball rapidly, and this is the function of the racket swing: to put a mean "buzz" on the ball so it will jump or kick when it lands. Simultaneously the weight presses forward, straight behind the shot. This gives the ball enough pace so it will skid and kick low. It also starts the attacker toward the net. He presses the shot and keeps right on going. Thus, the follow-up is co-ordinated with and made a part of the shot (Figures 27–29, pages 56–57).

This crossing-the-ball swing needs to be dwelt upon. It is a strange concept to many people. They cannot stop themselves from drawing back. To reach the ball they must then swing forward. They get far too much length and their shot continually sails out. They feel if they just prepare out and swing in the ball won't go. If they don't move their weight, this is true. But the combination of cutting in with the racket and pushing forward with the weight has a composite effect: The arm is cutting almost straight across, but is being carried forward by the moving body as it does so. Thus, the final result of the two motions put together is a diagonally forward-and-across motion of the racket. The difficult thing to learn is that the arm does not do the forward part—the weight does it. Actually, a slice without any weight (or almost none) is what we use for a drop shot: The ball hardly goes at all. It floats and barely gets past the net.

Players who have this difficulty can use a couple of tricks to train themselves. Try to swing rather sharply but make the ball go slowly. The only way to do it is to pull *off* the ball from the outside in. As long as you swing forward and put the racket through the ball, it will go fast. Another trick is to try to spin it sharply but make it land very short. In other words, exaggerate. Or, go to the extreme: Learn a drop shot and then push the shot (with the weight) deeper and deeper until it grows into an approach. However it is learned, it must be properly visualized as a pull with the racket and a push with the weight. Think of reaching out sideways for a rope and then hauling it in and across in front of you. That is roughly a slice swing. On a backhand slice the elbow will kick out to the right on the follow-through.

It is important *not* to use wrist. The racket is pulled through or dragged behind the arm. It is not sent first. The butt of the racket leads all the way—the head never overtakes and comes around as it may, for instance, on a cross-court forehand topspin shot. Thus, there is little hit or strike. The strings are drawn across the back of the ball, they are not pushed forward through it. The weight does the pushing. It can be summed up by saying, "The racket spins the ball. The weight makes it go."

If this theme has been belabored, it is because so many people have no concept of what it means to slice. They think it merely means swing the same old way but cut the ball. They can't understand why some players can keep the slice in but they cannot. They hit forward through it, the backspin holds the ball in the air, it sails out. This frustration cannot be ameliorated until they amend their mental picture of what it is they are trying to do.

AIM SHORT

"Aim your approach shot deep" is a cliché that is often repeated and seldom questioned. It is actually open to serious question. When a player makes an approach shot he aims as far to one side as he dares in order to open the court for his subsequent volley. In so doing, he runs a calculated risk: He aims closer to the side line than he would aim an ordinary base-line drive. But if he also aims deep, he is now running a second risk: He may go beyond the base line. It is a very good maxim that says, "Never take more than one risk." If a player risks the side line, he should not also risk the base line. Two risks are one too many.

It will immediately be argued that a shorter shot will be less effective, less forcing. It is generally assumed that the deeper the shot the more forcing it is. But is it? A shot played deep cannot be angled more than to the deep corner. An opponent starting from good position behind the center of the base line can reach any such shot in two or three steps. The attacking shot goes *to* him, where he is; namely, behind the base line. By contrast, if the ball is aimed shorter, it can be angled more sharply without going out. It can be made to bounce across the side line rather than across the base line, thereby going further *away* from him, making him scramble farther, opening the court wider. Additionally, the ball will be lower when he reaches it, obliging him to hit up more, and this markedly increases the difficulty of a successful passing shot. If the setup is high to the forehand and is walloped down the line, it will be very forcing almost no matter what its depth. A hard-hit ball bounces hard. The bounce will be very forcing whether it lands two feet or ten feet inside the base line. And, again, if the setup is at all near the center rather than right on the side line, aiming shorter makes it possible to increase the angle on the attacking shot.

All this adds up to the fact that approach shots should be aimed *way in* in terms of depth, limiting the risk to the side line. A good general spot is three to five feet behind the service line. To many this will sound like heresy. They are invited to try it. A slice placed to this spot will be lower and farther to the side when played by the defender. Both a slice and a hard-hit ball placed to this spot can be made to carry an opponent completely out of court into the alley to make his return. The opening for the next shot is much enlarged, the defender's recovery problem is more severe, and the ball is lower when he plays it.

It has been mentioned that on an approach a player has less distance in front of him, so he tends to hit out, and that the forward move behind the shot tends to increase its depth, again increasing the risk of hitting out over the base line. If in addition he thinks, "I should aim very deep," he will surely hit out on many occasions, often half the time (a horrendously poor percentage). Aiming short tends to correct all three of these "out" tendencies.

Some may think the above is an exaggeration. It is not. It happens that the author has been a college coach for forty-four years. Each year a new group arrives: number one school players, usually some with sectional and occasionally national junior rankings. Surely these are "advanced" players. Yet, with few exceptions they all, year after year, hit their approach shots out and have to be trained to shorten them to keep them in. They all use a big base-line swing, aim deep, and hit over the base line an amazing amount. These players come from all over the country: California, Texas, Florida, Chicago, New York, New England. It therefore can be flatly stated that this tendency to overhit in the half-court area is country wide and should receive much more emphasis than it has to date.

Rather than doubt this theoretical approach some may accept it enthusiastically and seek to carry it even farther. Why not aim for the corner of the service court? This increases the attacker's margins even more. But now the risk is too great. It is so easy to hit the top of the net or a foot into the alley. To go to this extreme is non-percentage. Three to five feet behind the service line is the best that can be achieved. It is the most pressure and difficulty that can be imposed on a defender while keeping the attacker's risk factor within reasonable bounds.

Individualism has a definite legitimate place in thinking about this problem. Someone who hits very hard should give himself a larger target by aiming farther in. He relies on the force of his shot rather than on its exact placement. Someone who is not a natural big hitter should go closer to the lines and achieve the best possible angle. He relies on keeping the ball very low and on moving his opponent farther. A very good rule is to take a big target when hitting hard, play more carefully for a small target, and never try for both— i.e., don't hit hard for a small target because you'll miss it too often.

These matters of percentage can be argued indefinitely because of the range of possibilities pointed out above. No rigid rule can be laid down. Each advanced player must find out for himself his own style, how far he can go in speed and accuracy, and the combination of both that best fits his talents, temperament, and skill. But it definitely can be stated that aiming short rather than long, thus bringing in the possibility of angling the ball, should be an important part of any player's thinking. The usual statement, "Aim your approach shots deep," is a very superficial blanket rule that is about as shallow an analysis as one could find.

THE DROP SHOT

This is a shot that practically disappeared from men's big time tennis. When every player followed his service to net on every occasion there was never an opportunity to use a drop shot. Recently, some major events (Longwood, Forest Hills, etc.) have returned to slower surfaces, and the drop shot is again an effective tool. However, it is noticeable that the drop shot was never discarded in women's tennis, nor did its usefulness diminish on the thousands of slow courts all over the East, Midwest, and South. Whether the top men's tennis uses it or not, the drop shot has been and will remain a shot so valuable that it can be termed indispensable to an all-round technique.

Tactically the drop shot has its chief value as a constant double threat. In performing this function it should be considered not as a shot that stands alone, but as one closely related to the approach shot. It is a half-court shot because it cannot be made effectively unless one is inside the base line. If it is attempted from the base line or behind it, the ball has too far to travel. Not only is it difficult to be sufficiently accurate over the greater distance, but also the defender has a significantly longer time to run in and attack in his turn. For these very good reasons the shot is seldom attempted unless the striker can move at least a couple of steps inside the base line to play the ball. He then has the choice of attacking with a standard approach shot or varying it with the drop shot.

How much to use the drop shot can vary quite drastically —it depends on several factors outside a player's control. On a very slow court, such as a clay court soon after rain, the more forceful attacking shots are slowed and their effectiveness reduced by the mattresslike bounce. By contrast, the drop shot is very dead and difficult to handle. Clearly it should be used with increased frequency. On a harder court the shot can be a pointless sacrifice, unless used infrequently so it has the element of surprise.

An opponent's skill or lack of it is often an important clue. If he is slow moving in and doesn't do much with the ball when he gets there, one can use a lot of drop shots with devastating results. Many steady baseliners are mediocre at handling a low ball up nearer the net. It can be said they can stand a lot of pressure but are easier victims when suction is substituted. One cannot seem to push them over backward, but it is not difficult to make them fall on their faces. Others come in pretty fast and handle the low ball adequately but are weak overhead. The well-known drop-followed-by-lob sequence can give them trouble. And, there is the wind. A drop against the wind is deadly; with the wind, usually hopeless.

Thus, it is not possible to lay down any hard-and-fast rules about the proper use of the drop shot, since the answer varies with the surface, the speed of the opponent, his skills, the weather, and even the speed of the ball being used. In general, it is more important on slow courts and less so on harder courts. But every advanced player should master the technique, so that on those occasions when it is most valuable he has it at his command. And even on a fast court a few should be used, just so the opponent knows he *can* and *might* drop it. This prevents a defender from hanging back to get more time against a hard shot. Just as the threat of the lob holds a net player back a bit, thus creating a little room at his feet or space for a passing shot, so the drop shot prevents the retreat that makes it hard to get pressure on him and gives him time to make a perfect lob instead of a hasty, shaky one. Using the drop shot as a means of making one's harder shots effective is often passed over quickly as a "change of pace." It is more than that. It suddenly attacks the front of the court instead of the back, and it presents the defender with a totally different problem, which he must continually worry about even if it is used only occasionally. Gar Mulloy, a great clay-court tactician, put it succinctly, "Oh yes, you have to use some drops, even if you lose those points, in order to make the rest of your shots go." Young players presently developing their offenses would do well to heed those words: Mulloy ranked in the first ten in the United States for twenty consecutive years. One may say this is a reasonable proof of consistent success. Mulloy had a very big forehand, yet if one dropped back a bit when he attacked with this formidable weapon, he was always quick to insert a little drop shot on the next chance. His use of his big forehand was an astute as it was forceful. That little drop shot made it even bigger.

DROP-SHOT TECHNIQUE

All the uses of the drop shot described in the preceding paragraphs constantly relate it to the other alternatives—the hard drive or kicking slice. In this context it is at once obvious that deception is of extreme importance. As in defensive play, deception depends on hiding the shot, and this is best achieved by cultivating identical preparation. This requires practice. The easiest road to success is always to prepare to play hard, then use only a small amount of the force that obviously could be applied. It is easy to use less of what one has ready; it is impossible to use more. If a player does not have his full array of power ready, the drop shot is easy to read and his opponent gets a beautiful head start.

A drop shot is primarily a vertical shot. It does not skim low over the net like a slice approach. It goes up from the racket to about twice the height of the net, then drops down just past it. In other words, it is a shot that drops. It should be falling when it crosses the net. If it is to fall down, it must first be played up.

Perhaps the foregoing seems obvious. Yet in years of teaching the author has found that eight or nine of any ten *advanced* players (not beginners) do not have this mental picture of a ball that goes quite sharply up from the racket then falls down. The majority always aim a low skimmer that either falls into the net or travels over level so its second bounce is well behind the service line. This is a setup, not a drop shot (Figures 39, 40).

The ball should be played with quite a bit of slice, achieved by drawing the racket across the ball. If as this is done the player also curls under the ball, it will pop up, fall down, and stay right where it lands: The spin will prevent a forward bounce. Most players can learn this quite easily, but their ball still goes too deep. They drop it nicely, somewhere near the service line! This is because they have too much swing. There must be *no* swing. The ball should come to the racket, not the racket to the ball. This means there should be *no* backswing, since if the racket is taken away it must be brought back—and this is what is not wanted since it will produce depth. If a player puts his racket *to* the ball—the exact opposite of a backswing—and just feathers (crosses) the

The Drop Shot 39

Note that Figure 39 is identical with The Approach Shot, page 125. From that same preparation, which threatens a power attack, the player can merely chop the ball and stop at Figure 40, having executed a neat chip drop shot. The most important

ball with the racket so the ball only goes three or four feet, he will have the idea and the feel. If, to this tickling, feather "stroke" he adds just enough leg push to float the ball to the net, so it just barely makes it, he will get a good drop.

The secret of learning it is to do less and less not more and more. Less and less approach swing, less and less hit,

aspect of this technique is to make the preparation identical with that for hard approach shots, so an opponent cannot read your intent.

less and less weight—until at last one gets that little tweaky nothing ball, a deadly drop shot. It helps to exaggerate. Try to pop the ball up so gently and short that it falls down on top of the net. In other words, try to make a lucky net-cord ball that just rolls over to the other side. This quickly shows what great restraint is needed to make a truly short shot on purpose.

Surley someone will ask, where is all this deception and identical preparation? If a player does what is described above, will he not look entirely different, thus giving it all away? Not if he does it correctly. He should set up quickly, racket to the side (*not* back), feet set, shoulders turned so it is clear he *could* really sock the ball or slice it severely. But he doesn't. From that coiled position that threatens the big one, he unleashes only a very small fraction of the latent prepared power, and out pops a little drop shot.

TOUCH MEANS FIRMNESS

Many players have a mistaken concept of what is meant by "finesse" or "touch." When attempting any soft shot (drop, drop volley, lob) they relax their grip. A slop shot, not a drop shot, usually results. Delicacy means strength used with controlled restraint. A loose grip gives weakness and lack of control: the opposite of finesse. A soft shot such as a drop must be *exact*. This requires a very firm grip for total control and very little, if any, wrist—except to turn a bit under the ball (frequently called "cupping").

The length on a drop shot is controlled by the legs. A player pushes the ball just so far and no farther. The firm grip on the racket transfers this push to the ball. A loose grip gives way to the ball: The ball tells the racket instead of the racket telling the ball. The shot is floppy, sloppy, uncontrolled. Worse, relaxation is usually a dead giveaway. The defender quickly spots the fact that the attacker is going to play softly. This means he anticipates and is in there for a kill. Therefore, both control and deception demand that we prepare as though for a major effort, and that we keep a firm grip as we play the ball. A good analogy is "threading a needle." Try to thread a needle holding the thread loosely in one hand and the needle loosely in the other. You can't do it. You must hold them firmly and bring them *exactly* together. It is the same with a finesse shot.

VII

Conclusions

A PERSPECTIVE ON GROUND STROKES

If the analysis presented in this book has validity, then it is a fact that the usual concept of ground strokes is far too limited. It confines itself, for the most part, to the base-line rally and tacitly assumes that if this technique is mastered, then other applications of ground strokes will automatically be taken care of by extension. The whole point of the book is to assert, and hopefully to prove, that this assumption is unsound and results in grave shortcomings in the techniques of players who may be quite sound on the base line.

It is valid to assert that the first skill a beginner and intermediate must learn is to keep the ball in play and become reasonably successful in the base-line rally. It is not valid to continue endlessly polishing this skill to the total neglect of the other skills; namely, defensive play and half-court shots. Often when this complaint is made, someone will reply that there isn't time to practice these "other" things, and it is unfair to demand so much. Yet if one has a group of advanced players and asks, "How many have practiced the overhead as a specific separate skill?" *every* player will raise his hand. Then ask, "How many have practiced approach shots and the drop shot as specific separate skills?" Only about one in eight or ten will lift a hand; sometimes none. Everybody seems to have plenty of time to practice the overhead because they recognize its importance. The reason they do not practice defense and half-court shots is not time, but because they do not perceive these skills as needing separate attention.

It is very common to see two players rally from the base line, and to see each allow the ball to bounce twice if the other hits a shot short. It never occurs to them that here is a chance to practice moving in and playing a half-court shot, and that they *need* this practice as much as they need baseline practice. Probably more. And how often do we see players work on developing a deceptive passing shot? Practically never. Yet all, without fail, drill their volley, their overhead, and base-line drives, every day ad infinitum. No, it is not lack of time; it is lack of perspective. If a player realizes that here is a skill he needs, just as he needs a volley and an overhead, he will practice that skill. He will make time for it, work on it, and perfect it. He will become more well rounded.

Attention is drawn to the offense-defense drill: The server must serve underhand and give the receiver a short ball, the receiver must attack, the server defend. If this drill is co-ordinated with drills on individual shots, it will go far toward filling the gaps in tactical and technical skills that are so prevalent in advanced players today.

SOMETHING ABOUT DRILLS

One of the most common requests at seminars for teachers or advanced players is for suggestions for good drills. Many seem to think that there is something secret or special about a good drill. Actually, all any drill amounts to is to isolate some specific skill and repeat it again and again. For example, two players trade backhands continually to drill their cross-court backhand skill. One player may want to perfect his topspin serve to the backhand. Another is weak on backhand return of service. Put them together: The server serves to the backhand, the receiver practices his return. To teach a drop shot, place the pupil behind the base line, feed him short setups. He moves in and drops the ball. Teach the approach shot the same way, but divide it into four categories: low and high forehand, low and high backhand. Drill each separately. After a player has learned the individual shots, the offense-defense game gives him varied practice. The main principle in drilling is to pick out and separate the aspect of technique that is giving trouble. The drill merely limits play to repeating that particular thing many times. Anyone can make up a drill for any skill at any time.

Often special advanced combination drills are exhibited at seminars and conferences. These are exciting and entertaining to watch, and some are led to believe these drills are therefore superior or to be preferred. Actually, most of these are tempo drills, such as two on one, where two net players run a baseliner from side to side just as fast as he can go. These aid in recovery speed, quick preparation, fast starts, etc. They do *not* teach individual racket skills in the sense of learning a backhand or a forehand. They teach quickness at something one has supposedly already learned. These tempo drills are very good for developing quickness and agility. They are not good for developing racket skills, and there should be no confusion as to their function. It can be a mistake to rush into a tempo drill before a player can do it slowly without pressure.

A very entertaining drill—good only for very advanced

players who can execute it—is to have one player up, the other back. The net player plays first to one side, then the other, forcing the baseliner from side to side. The baseliner alternately drives and lobs, so the net player moves up, back, up, back. Such a drill puts on a fine show and is very good for both players *provided* they are advanced enough to keep it going without constant interruption due to errors. While we all can admire such a drill, it is irrelevant to the current needs of most players.

Less spectacular but usually more profitable practice for most of us are drills that drum into a player one specific skill. For example: exchange cross-courts. This need not be as dull as it sounds. It is easy to make it a game: Whoever makes an error or puts the ball in the wrong half of the court loses the point. Set the game at any level desired—ten points, twenty points. As players improve, make it tougher: Every ball must land behind the service line in the correct half. (If you think this is a cinch, just try it. But remember, this is what every tough baseliner should be able to do.) Further variation can be achieved by stipulating that every shot must be a topspin, or every shot a slice. Thus, even the most basic base-line ground strokes can be drilled in a manner that gives pleasure and variety while focusing one's attention on a specific skill.

It helps to have a drill progression in mind. Such a progression should start with the crudest use of strokes: the base-line rally with the whole court as the target. Then it can move to the cross-court: half the court as target. Then to the deep cross-court: one quarter of the court as target (behind the service line on one side). These three drills carry the base-line rally from the beginner stage to the consistent depth stage.

For defensive drives against a net player, the first skill to be taught is more than normal topspin so the ball dips sharply and lands short. A very good drill is to place a net player in a slightly vulnerable position—a quarter or a third of the way from the service line to the net—and have him volley to a base-line player. The deep player should try to put enough spin on the ball to force him to half volley or make a very low volley. This, of course, is also an excellent drill for the net player, teaching him to make the most difficult low shots at net. The base-line player at first plays pretty much to the center, concentrating on the spin and the conscious avoidance of depth. After this trick is reasonably mastered, he can try placing it to either side. The final (third) stage of refinement is to perfect the quick short preparation, identical whether he intends to play straight or cross-court or lob, and the sudden sharp release that maximizes deception.

For half-court shots the first objective on the backhand is the ability to make a sharply spinning slice that stays in the court when played off a short ball. The second stage is to place it close to the side lines, not too deep. The third stage, as usual, is to incorporate deceptive preparation and release, so the defender cannot guess whether the attack will be straight, cross-court, or drop. On the forehand a player usually develops a wallop on a high setup and a mean slice for a low ball.

All these drills lead up to the offense-defense game previously described, wherein there is no service, return of service, or base-line rally, and play consists entirely of attack and defense. While service and net play are not the subjects of this book, this game is equally effective in perfecting the use of many of those skills: position play at net, all sorts of volleys, and the overhead.

Emphasis on this apparently queer way to play tennis has been extreme in this book because it forces on players those aspects of the game that as a rule are almost totally neglected. Customarily players warm up from the base line, hit some at net, ask for some lobs, hit some serves, and announce, "I'm ready." They have not hit *one* approach, drop, or passing shot. Then they play. There is constant serving, return of serving, and if on clay there are constant base-line exchanges. Only intermittently is there the chance for the approach, drop, or passing shot. Yet when they occur they are crucial shots. They decide points. So even after playing several sets these important techniques will have received only a little attention. The serve-a-setup game is therefore not just an entertaining way of practicing. It is actually a method of concentrating play on those areas that are important but do not occur often enough in regular play to sharpen them to excellence.

Perhaps a single example will reinforce this perspective convincingly. In the fine Connors-Borg final in the 1976 U. S. Open at Forest Hills they each won a set. In the third set Connors had an edge in the powerful base-line exchanges, but when he provoked a short return, attacked it, and moved in, his approach shots were shaky. He made some errors that were meat for Borg's fine passes. The set went to a hair-raising tie breaker and Connors was lucky to win it. In the fourth set, Connors made excellent wide approaches, few errors, and won decisively. The difference was in these attacking shots. Borg refused to come to net except when drawn so far in he couldn't retreat. Connors attacked the net whenever he had a chance. The quality of his attack was the deciding factor. Winning the rally wasn't enough: He had to follow that up with great skill to overcome Borg's defensive skill. His approach shots were keen in the final set, and suddenly it was no longer a close match.

Of course, few can rally with the consistent power that characterizes these top players. But this is not the point, which is that whenever two players are fairly even in the exchange, the one who can best capitalize on his opportunities comes out on top. The principle holds true at any level of excellence, not merely in the finals of the U. S. Open.

It is hoped that this book will stimulate a broader concept of ground strokes, that players and teachers will think of them in relation to all three categories (base-line rally, defense, attack), and that discussion and perhaps interesting controversy in these areas will become far more prevalent than heretofore.

With the co-operation of the United States Tennis Association, Doubleday & Company, Inc., has published the following titles in this series:

SPEED, STRENGTH, AND STAMINA: CONDITIONING FOR TENNIS, by Connie Haynes with Steven Kraft and John Conroy.
Detailed descriptions of exercises for tennis players and suggestions for keeping in shape.

TACTICS IN WOMEN'S SINGLES, DOUBLES, AND MIXED DOUBLES, by Rex Lardner.
A book for women tennis players, with specific suggestions for taking advantage of opponents' weaknesses.

SINISTER TENNIS, by Peter Schwed.
How to play against left-handers, and also with left-handers as doubles partners.

RETURNING THE SERVE INTELLIGENTLY, by Sterling Lord.
How you can reduce errors, minimize the server's advantage, and launch your own attack.

COVERING THE COURT, by Edward T. Chase.
How to be a winning court coverer and keep maximum pressure on your opponent.

FINDING AND EXPLOITING YOUR OPPONENT'S WEAKNESSES, by Rex Lardner.

THE SERVE AND THE OVERHEAD SMASH, by Peter Schwed.
How the intermediate player can best hit the big shots.

THE VOLLEY AND THE HALF-VOLLEY: THE ATTACKING GAME, by John F. Kenfield.

TENNIS DRILLS FOR SELF-IMPROVEMENT, edited by Steven Kraft, USTA Education and Research Center.
Ten of the nation's top young tennis coaches offer forty-two favorite drills.

GROUND STROKES IN MATCH PLAY: TECHNIQUES, TEMPO, AND WINNING TACTICS, by Jack Barnaby.

THE TENNIS PLAYER'S DIET: A GUIDE TO BETTER NUTRITION ON AND OFF THE COURT, by Connie Haynes and Steven Kraft.